Collins

WJEC Eduqas GCSE 9-1

T0364347

English Language & Literature

Workbook

Paul Burns

Contents

Contents

Nineteenth-Century Prose

Practice Exam Papers

Key Technical Skills: Writing

Spelling

1 Put the following words into their plural forms:

a) tomato .... b) birthday ....

c) soliloquy .... d) family ....

e) parenthesis .... [5]

2 Insert the correctly spelled word in each of the following pairs of sentences:

a) **Your/you're**

.... not going out like that.

I asked .... sister to bring it.

b) **There/they're/their**

.... are twenty people in the class.

They have all done ....

homework but .... not

sitting in the right places.

c) **Where/wear/we're**

Turn it off or it will .... out.

We have no idea .... it is but

.... going anyway.

d) **Past/passed**

I .... him in the street

an hour ago.

He walked right .... me

as if I wasn't there.

e) **To/too/two**

There were only ....

exams .... sit but that

was one .... many.

f) **Practice/practise**

If you don't go to the .... you'll

be left out of the team.

If you want to improve you will have to

.... every day. [15]

3 The following passage includes ten incorrect spellings. Find them and circle them, then write the correct spellings below.

> Last nite I went to the cinema with my friend Bob and his farther, Michael. The whole evening was not very succesfull. The cinema was very crouded and we had to sit seperately. Then, it turned out the film was in a forrein langauge and no-one could understand it. I think it was about the enviroment. Afterwards, Michael took us to a resturant were we had pizzas.

....

....

....

....

....

[10]

Total Marks .... / 30

Key Technical Skills: Writing

1 Punctuate the following passage using only commas and full stops. There should be a total of five punctuation marks. You may wish to rewrite the passage to add the punctuation.

> *Great Expectations* one of the best-known novels by Charles Dickens is the story of Pip a boy who grows up in the marshes of Kent at the beginning of the story he meets an escaped convict in the churchyard where his parents are buried

[5]

2 Add ten apostrophes, where necessary, to the following passage. You may wish to rewrite the passage to add the apostrophes.

> At about ten o clock, we went to Romios for pizzas. Im not sure what Bobs pizza topping was but I had ham and pineapple. I wish I hadnt because later on I was sick in Michaels car. Its brand new and I thought hed be angry but he wasnt. Were not going there again.

[10]

3 Add a question mark, an exclamation mark, a colon, a semi-colon or parentheses (brackets) to the following clauses so that they make sense:

a) The cat slept quietly on the mat the dog slept noisily on the step.	
b) Who was that masked man nobody knows.	
c) I don't believe it that's the first answer I've got.	
d) Annie deserved the prize she was the best baker by far.	
e) Jane and Elizabeth the two oldest Bennet sisters get married at the end.	

[5]

Total Marks _____ / 20

Key Technical Skills: Writing

Sentence Structure

1 Identify whether the sentences below are simple, compound, complex or minor sentences:

   a) I confess that I had my doubts when I reflected upon the great traffic which had passed along the London road in the interval. ....

   b) Very clearly. ....

   c) We all need help sometimes. ....

   d) Mr Collins was punctual to his time, and he was received with great politeness by the whole family. ....

   e) Elizabeth smiled. ....   [5]

2 Combine the following sentences to form complex sentences, using the conjunctions **because**, **although** or **until**.

   a) I bought Anna a bunch of flowers. It was her birthday.

       ....

       ....

   b) He did not finish the race. They gave him a certificate.

       ....

       ....

   c) I kept going. I reached the finishing line.

       ....

       ....   [3]

3 Use the following sentences to form a complex sentence using a relative pronoun.
   Joey was the oldest cat in the street. He never left the garden.

   ....

   ....

   ....   [1]

4 Use the following sentences to form a complex sentence without using a connective:
   I was walking down the street. I realised I had forgotten my phone.

   ....

   ....

   ....   [1]

Total Marks .... / 10

Key Technical Skills: Writing

Text Structure and Organisation

1 Rearrange the following paragraphs from 1 to 5 so that the passage makes sense.

a) As a result of this, the student body has decided to appeal to the governors. Jodie has written a letter to every governor, setting out the problems as the students see them. ☐

b) As yet no replies have been received. The increasingly angry students are starting to consider taking 'direct action'. ☐

c) Jodie Collins, a spokesperson for the students, has had several meetings about the issue with the Principal. Ms Rundle apparently listened to the students' points, but later sent an email claiming that nothing can be done because of lack of funds. ☐

d) According to this letter, students' health and safety are at risk. Among other things, toilets are not properly cleaned and standards of hygiene in the kitchen leave a lot to be desired. ☐

e) Students of Summerfield College have expressed concern about the environment they have to work in. They have a number of complaints. ☐

[5]

2 Insert each of these five discourse markers or connectives into the passage so that it makes sense:

| nevertheless | when | subsequently | in spite of | however |

(a) .... I read your letter I was shocked by its contents.

(b) .... being a governor of the college, I was completely unaware of

the issues that you mention. I have (c) .... been in touch with Ms Rundle

to express my concern. She (d), ..., has not responded to my letters.

(e) ...., I shall continue to press her for answers. [5]

Key Technical Skills: Writing

Standard English and Grammar

1 Insert the correct form of the verb 'to be' or 'to do':

Present tense

a) You .... a great singer.

b) They .... trying hard.

Simple past

c) We .... waiting for you.

d) He .... what they told him to do.

Perfect

e) She .... my friend for years.

f) They .... all their exams now.

Simple past + past perfect

g) We .... happy because we .... all the exercises.   [7]

2 Which of the following is correct in Standard UK English? Circle the correct word.

a) The defendant **pleaded/pled** guilty.

b) He's one of the **only/few** people who can do that.

c) He has **got/gotten** two coffees.   [3]

3 Change the following dialogue to Standard English:

Jo: Hey. How are you guys doing? ....

Arthur: Good. Real good. ....

Jo: Wanna drink? ....

Arthur: Can I get two coffees? ....

Jo: Sure. Where are you sat? ....   [5]

4 Rewrite the following passage in Standard English:

> I was stood in the street when Frankie come over. I give him a smile and opened me gob to speak. I was gonna ask him how he done in math. I never said nothing. Soon as I seen him I knew he done good.

....

....

....

....   [5]

Total Marks .... / 20

Key Technical Skills: Reading

1 Read the passage below:

> The tower of St Peter's church was, until very recently, the tallest building in the town. On a clear day, it can still be seen from miles away. However, it is now overshadowed by a brutal example of modern architecture. Built two years ago, and twice as high as the church tower, the Kingsley Tower dominates the surrounding landscape.

Look at the statements below. Which of them are explicitly stated in the text? Tick the correct answers.

a) The church tower used to be the tallest building in town. ☐

b) Everyone hates the new building. ☐

c) The Kingsley Tower is taller than the church tower. ☐

d) The writer does not like modern architecture. ☐ [2]

2 Read the passage below:

List five things that we learn about the old gentleman's appearance.

> It was by the Green Dragon that the old gentleman travelled. He was a very nice looking old gentleman, and he looked as if he were nice, too, which is not at all the same thing. He had a fresh-coloured, clean-shaven face, and white hair, and he wore rather odd-shaped collars and a top hat that wasn't exactly the same kind as other people's. Of course the children didn't see all this at first. In fact, the first thing they noticed about the old gentleman was his hand.
>
> From *The Railway Children* by E. Nesbit

....

....

....

....

....

....

....

....

[5]

Total Marks .... / 7

Key Technical Skills: Reading

Identifying Information and Ideas 2

1 Read the passage and answer the questions below.

> Work experience is an established part of today's school calendar. All Year 10 pupils in all schools have to do it. But why? I decided to ask around and found the general opinion amongst the adults I asked was that it would prepare young people for the world of work. I have to say, though, that none of them sounded terribly convinced and I got the distinct impression that they were just following the party line.
>
> Assuming the object of the exercise is to prepare us for the world of work, does it? My placement was in my uncle's office. He is a solicitor and the rationale behind the placement was that I had expressed an interest in studying Law. That sounds logical. But what did I learn? I learned that you should dress smartly and be punctual. I learned how to answer the telephone politely. I learned that solicitors drink an awful lot of coffee. I could have found out all of that just by having a chat with my uncle.

a) In which school year is work experience compulsory?

.... [1]

b) In the writer's opinion, do adults say what they really think about work experience?

.... [1]

c) What job does the writer's uncle do?

.... [1]

d) Name one thing the writer did while on work experience.

.... [1]

e) Did the writer find the experience valuable?

.... [1]

Total Marks .... / 5

Key Technical Skills: Reading

Summary

1 Reduce each of the following sentences to five words to give the necessary information without losing sense.

a) Stunning trees stand like soldiers behind the shed.	
b) Charlotte Green, the girl with blonde hair, ate Lydia's chocolate.	
c) I demand that you tell me now who did it.	

[3]

2 Read this statement from the witness to a crime.

> I was walking down our street – Arbuckle Lane – at nine o'clock on Monday. I know it was nine o'clock because I was worried about being late for work and I looked at my watch. As I passed number eighteen, the big house with the yellow front door where Mrs Lightbody used to live, I heard a noise, so I stopped and turned around. There were two men on the step and one of them had something in his hand, which he was using to break the glass in the door. I shouted out and they turned. One of them was tall, about six foot, with a grey beard – he reminded me of someone on the television – and the other one was stocky with curly black hair. When they saw me the tall man dropped something and they both ran. It gave me quite a turn.

If you were investigating the crime, which FIVE of the following pieces of information would be relevant to solving it? Tick the correct answers.

a) Mrs Lightbody lived at number eighteen. ☐

b) One of the men was six foot tall. ☐

c) He used something to break the glass in the door. ☐

d) The witness was worried about being late. ☐

e) The witness lives in Arbuckle Lane. ☐

f) The tall man dropped something. ☐

g) One man had curly black hair. ☐

h) It was nine o'clock. ☐ [5]

3 On a separate piece of paper, write a summary of the statement. Aim for 70 words or fewer. [12]

Total Marks _____ / 20

Key Technical Skills: Reading

1 Read the two passages below.

Pick out as many differences as you can between the two girls' experiences of school and write them in the table below or on a separate piece of paper.

> **Mary Jane:** I grew up on a farm near Barrow. My parents were not at all happy about me going to school, but they were told it was the law and I had to go. They couldn't see the point of it. But I loved school and I never missed a day. The school was a low stone building in the centre of the village. There were two huge rooms, one for the juniors and one for the infants. There were forty pupils in my class and we sat in rows, facing the teacher. We worked really hard all day, except for playtime, and we were not allowed to speak at all unless spoken to. Miss Murdishaw was very strict. We did like her, though, and she only gave you the cane if you were very naughty.
>
> **Sarah:** I would never have gone to school at all if I'd had my way. But I was never allowed to stay off. 'Education, education, education', my mum used to say, 'that's what you need in life. Miss a day's school and you'll regret it'. My first school was in the village near where we lived. There were twenty-four children in our class and we used to sit around tables in groups of six. All my group did was talk, talk, talk all day long. I don't think we did much work at all. The teacher just wandered around the room smiling at us and telling us everything we did was brilliant. She never punished anyone really, not even telling them off. I think she thought we all loved her, but I certainly didn't.

Mary Jane	Sarah

[10]

2 Now sum up the differences between the girls' experiences of school, writing in proper sentences.

....

....

....

....

[4]

Total Marks .... / 14

Key Technical Skills: Reading

1 Match each statement (**a–c**) with its paraphrase (**d–f**):

a) The modern apartments are situated close to all amenities.

b) Six o'clock struck on the bells of the church that was so conveniently near to the solicitor's dwelling, and still he was digging at the problem.

c) She suggested liaising outside the church at 18.05. I said yes.

d) The lawyer was still trying to work it out in the evening.

e) The flats are up-to-date and near shops and transport.

f) We agreed to meet at about six o'clock by the church.

[3]

2 The following sentences all include quotations from *Macbeth* which have not been set out correctly. Set them out correctly, using colons and/or quotation marks where appropriate.

a) Macbeth refers to the prophecies as happy prologues.	
b) He tells us that one of them has come true I am Thane of Cawdor.	
c) Macbeth asks how the prophecies can be evil when the witches have told the truth If ill, Why hath it given me earnest of success/Commencing in a truth?	

[6]

3 The following sentences are an example of the use of PEE. Identify the point, the evidence and the explanation.

Frankenstein's response is negative from the start. Referring to the experiment as a 'catastrophe' and his creation as a 'wretch' suggests that he has rejected the creature and will not try to find any good in it.

Point	
Evidence	
Explanation	

[3]

Total Marks _____ / 12

Key Technical Skills: Reading

Analysing Language 1

1 How would you describe the register of the following sentences?

Choose from:

formal

technical

dialectical

colloquial

a) 'Appen he were took badly but he'll be all reet. ....

b) It may be that the gentleman was feeling ill. It is, however, likely that he will recover.

....

c) Me mate wasn't feeling too good but he's OK now. ....

d) The patient suffered a brief episode of disequilibrium, which could be a symptom of a number of chronic conditions.

....

[4]

2 Read the passage below and identify the word class (part of speech) of the highlighted words:

> Since the party, she had been more **eager** than ever, and had planned many ways of making friends **with** him; **but** he had not been seen lately, and Jo began to think he had gone away, when she one day spied a brown face at an upper **window**, looking **wistfully** down into their garden, where Beth and Amy **were snowballing** one another.
>
> From *Little Women* by Louisa May Alcott

a) eager		b) with	
c) but		d) window	
e) wistfully		f) were snowballing	

[6]

3 a) The passage above is only one sentence. What sort of sentence is it? ....

b) Give an example from the passage of a proper noun. ....

c) Is the clause 'he had not been seen lately' in the active or passive voice? ....

d) What tense is 'had planned' in the first line? ....

e) In what 'person' is the narrative written? ....

[5]

Total Marks .... / 15

Key Technical Skills: Reading

1 State whether each of the following sentences contains a metaphor or a simile and describe the effect of the comparison.

	Metaphor or simile?	What is its effect?
a) He ran like the wind.		
b) An army of insects invaded the kitchen.		
c) Her heart was as cold as ice.		

[6]

2 Read the passage below. Find an example of each of the techniques listed in the table below.

> Time was not on their side. The fire fizzed and crackled around them as the brave
> Brown brothers entered the building. Inside, great flames came in waves.

a) personification	
b) onomatopoeia	

[2]

3 Read the passage below, from *The Hound of the Baskervilles* by Arthur Conan Doyle.

> October 16th – A dull and foggy day, with a drizzle of rain. The house is banked with rolling clouds, which rise now and then to show the dreary curves of the moor, with thin, silver veins upon the sides of the hills, and the distant boulders gleaming where the light strikes upon their wet faces. It is melancholy outside and in. The baronet is in a black reaction after the excitements of the night. I am conscious myself of a weight at my heart and a feeling of impending danger – ever-present, which is the more terrible because I am unable to define it.
>   And have I not cause for such a feeling?

What impressions does the writer create of the narrator's thoughts and feelings?

You must refer to the language used in the text to support your answer. [5]
(Write your answer on a separate piece of paper.)

Total Marks _____ / 13

Key Technical Skills: Reading

Analysing Form and Structure

1 Here is the opening of a short story (*The Count and the Wedding Guest* by O. Henry).

> One evening when Andy Donovan went to dinner at his Second Avenue boarding-house, Mrs Scott introduced him to a new boarder, a young lady, Miss Conway. Miss Conway was small and unobtrusive. She wore a plain, snuffy-brown dress, and bestowed her interest, which seemed languid, upon her plate. She lifted her diffident eyelids and shot one perspicuous, judicial glance at Mr Donovan, politely murmured his name, and returned to her mutton. Mr Donovan bowed with the grace and beaming smile that were rapidly winning for him social, business and political advancement, and erased the snuffy-brown one from the tablets of his consideration.

a) What do we learn about the story's setting?

.... [2]

b) What is your first impression of Miss Conway?

.... [2]

c) What is the effect of the phrase 'shot one perspicuous, judicial glance'?

.... [2]

d) What does the description of Andy Donovan's response tell us about him?

.... [2]

e) What do you think might happen next?

.... [2]

2 Match the endings **a–c** with the descriptions **x–z**.

a) Honour the charge they made! Honour the Light Brigade, Noble six hundred!	**x)** This ending draws a lesson from the story.
b) ...the wishes, the hopes, the confidence, the predictions of the small band of true friends who witnessed the ceremony, were fully answered in the perfect happiness of the union.	**y)** This ending might inspire the reader.
c) 'Was I not right?' said the little Mouse. Little friends may prove great friends.	**z)** A happy ending, leaving the reader satisfied.

[3]

Total Marks .... / 13

English Language 1

1. Read the extracts below and state which is narrated by:

A naive/unreliable narrator	
An omniscient narrator	
A reliable first-person narrator	
An intrusive narrator	

[8]

A She told me to pray every day, and whatever I asked for I would get it. But it warn't so. I tried it. Once I got a fish-line but no hooks. It warn't any good to me without hooks. I tried for hooks three or four times, but somehow I couldn't make it work.

From The Adventures of Huckleberry Finn by Mark Twain

B The extract from my private diary which forms the last chapter has brought my narrative up to the 18th of October, a time when these strange events began to move swiftly towards their terrible conclusion.

From The Hound of the Baskervilles by Sir Arthur Conan Doyle

C As John Bold will occupy much of our attention, we must endeavour to explain who he is, and why he takes the part of John Hiram's beadsmen.

From The Warden by Anthony Trollope

D Mr James Duffy lived in Chapelizod because he wished to live as far as possible from the city of which he was a citizen and because he found all the other suburbs of Dublin mean, modern and pretentious.

From Dubliners by James Joyce

Total Marks _____ / 8

English Language 1

1 Look at the quotations in the table. In the third column (or on a separate piece of paper) enter **how we learn about character**, choosing from:

a) Narrator's description

b) What the character says

c) What others say about/to the character

d) What the character does

e) How others react to the character

In the fourth column (or on a separate piece of paper) say **what we learn about the character**.

Character	Quotation	How we learn about the character	What we learn
Hyde's housekeeper *The Strange Case of Dr Jekyll and Mr Hyde*	She had an evil face, smoothed by hypocrisy; but her manners were excellent.		
Magwitch *Great Expectations*	'Hold your noise!' cried a terrible voice [...] 'Keep still, you little devil, or I'll cut your throat.'		
Darcy *Pride and Prejudice*	[Darcy] was looked at with great admiration for about half the evening, till his manners gave a disgust which turned the tide of his popularity.		
Mrs Reed *Jane Eyre*	Mrs Reed, impatient of my now frantic anguish and wild sobs, abruptly thrust me back and locked me in...		
Victor Frankenstein *Frankenstein*	'My dear Victor,' cried he, 'what, for God's sake, is the matter? Do not laugh in that manner. How ill you are!'		

[15]

Total Marks _____ / 15

English Language 1

Creative Writing 1

Imagine you have been set the following creative writing task:

Write a story about someone who wins a huge amount of money on the lottery.

Use the following questions and points to help you create a plan for your writing.

1 Character and Voice

a) What person will you write in? If first person, is the narrator also the protagonist?

_____

b) What kind of register will the narrator use? _____

Now make notes on your protagonist's:

c) gender _____

d) age _____

e) appearance _____

f) background _____

g) relationships _____

h) way of speaking _____

i) interests _____

j) opinions _____ [10]

2 Place and Time

a) Where does it start? _____

b) Does the setting change during the story? _____

c) When is it set – now, in the past or in the future? ____

d) How long does the story take? _____

e) Will it be written in chronological order? _____ [5]

3 Structure

On a separate piece of paper, make notes on your:

a) exposition

b) inciting incident

c) turning point(s)

d) climax

e) coda (ending) [5]

Total Marks _____ / 20

English Language 1

Creative Writing 2

You have decided to describe:

a character in your story **and** a scene where part of your story takes place.

1 Give a name to:

Your character ....

The place .... [2]

2 The Five Senses

Using an adjective and a noun for each, in the table below jot down at least two things you can sense:

Sense	Character	Scene
a) see		
b) hear		
c) smell		
d) taste	Not applicable	
e) touch/feel		

[10]

3 Big to Small

Make notes on the scene/person from:

	Character	Scene
a) long distance		
b) middle distance		
c) close up		

[6]

4 Imagery

Write down an appropriate:

	Character	Scene
a) simile		
b) metaphor		

[2]

Total Marks .... / 20

English Language 2

1 Read the following short texts and use the table below to list differences in the writers' points of view and how they are expressed.

A

It's easy to miss Little Mickledon. It's a tiny village, with no shop or pub, nestling in a valley surrounded by fields of grazing sheep. It's a bit like stepping back in time to the Olde England of yore. It's charming and tranquil, cut off from 'civilization' by having no broadband and no mobile phone signal. But for visitors to Alf and Maisie's delightful bed and breakfast, that's a big attraction. 'People come here to relax', beams Maisie, 'and to rediscover a sense of inner peace and calm.'

B

The Bideaway B & B, Little Mickledon, was a massive disappointment. We were promised peace and quiet, sure, but we didn't expect to be totally cut off from the modern world. Be warned. There's no broadband and we couldn't get a mobile signal. When we complained – not our only complaint: the rooms were grubby and the breakfast pitiful – the hippy owners just shrugged their shoulders.

	Text A	Text B
What is the writer's attitude to Little Mickledon?		
What is the writer's opinion of the B & B?		
What impression do you get of the writer?		
How would you describe the general tone and style?		
Comment on language features.		

[20]

English Language 2

1 Imagine you have been asked to give your opinion on the statement 'Work Experience is a complete waste of time and should be abolished'.

Use the table below to list five arguments in favour of abolishing work experience (pro) and five against it (con).

Pros	Cons

[10]

2 The statement above was made in an article in your local newspaper. Decide whether you agree or disagree with it and write **the opening paragraph** of a letter to the newspaper expressing your view.

_____

_____

_____

_____

_____

[5]

3 Now write **the opening paragraph** of an article for a teenage magazine expressing your views on the same statement.

_____

_____

_____

_____

_____

[5]

Total Marks _____ / 20

Shakespeare

Context and Themes

1 Think about the Shakespeare play you have studied and write a sentence to explain how each of the following aspects of social and historical context is reflected in it.

a) The play's setting — **Example: *Romeo and Juliet* is set in Italy, a country associated with romance and feuding families.**

_____

_____

b) History and politics

_____

_____

c) Religion

_____

d) Society

_____

e) Gender roles

_____

f) Cultural context

_____ [12]

2 Think about the play you have studied and write a sentence explaining how each of the following themes is reflected in it.

a) Marriage — Example: **In *Romeo and Juliet* Capulet sees it as his right and duty to choose Juliet's husband, but Romeo and Juliet see marriage as an expression of love.**

_____

b) Appearance and reality

_____

c) Power

_____

d) Revenge

_____

e) Loyalty and betrayal

_____

f) Parents and children

_____ [12]

Total Marks _____ / 24

Shakespeare

Characters, Language and Structure

1 Choose at least three characters from the play you have studied and find quotations (either something they say or something other characters say) which you feel tell us something about their characters.

Enter the characters' names and appropriate quotations, together with a brief explanation of what you think each quotation tells us, in a table like the one below on a separate piece of paper.

For example, if you have studied *The Merchant of Venice* you could start with:

Character	Quotation	What it tells us
Portia	If I live to be as old as Sybilla, I will die as chaste as Diana unless I be obtained by the manner of my father's will. (Act 1 Scene 2).	Portia reveals her sense of duty and love for her father, as well as her strength of character, using classical references which show her level of education.

[12]

2 Below are some quotations from Shakespeare which demonstrate his use of the following literary techniques: metaphor, oxymoron, pathetic fallacy / personification, rhetorical question.

For each quotation, state which technique is being used and explain its effect.

a) O brawling love, O loving hate (*Romeo and Juliet*, Act 1 Scene 1)

b) But since I am a dog, beware my fangs. (*The Merchant of Venice*, Act 3 Scene 3)

c) Can this Cock-pit hold/ the vasty fields of France? (*Henry V*, Prologue)

d) Rough quarries, rocks and hills, whose heads touch heaven. (*Othello*, Act 1 Scene 3)

	Technique	Effect
a)		
b)		
c)		
d)		

[12]

Total Marks _____ / 24

Poetry

Context and Themes

Context

Think about the social, historical and cultural context of the poems you have studied.

1 Match these descriptions of the context of poems to the appropriate poems.

a) This poem is rooted in the poet's Irish heritage. ....

b) The poem's language reflects the speaker's Asian heritage. ....

c) The poet uses a Petrarchan sonnet to express her feelings. ....

d) In this Romantic poem the poet learns from nature. ....

e) This poem is inspired by the finding of soldiers' remains in a field.

.... [5]

Themes

Now think about themes and ideas touched on in the poems you have studied.

2 Which poems touch on the following aspects of the main theme (love and relationships)? Try to find at least two for each. You may list the same poem under more than one heading:

a) The power of nature	
b) The beauty of nature	
c) City life	
d) Romantic love	
e) The experience of combatants (soldiers)	
f) The effect of war on non-combatants	
g) Childhood	
h) Memories	

[16]

Total Marks .... / 21

Poetry

Language, Form and Structure

1. Below are some lines taken from poems which demonstrate poets' use of various language choices and literary techniques.

   a) How do I love thee? Let me count the ways! (Sonnet 43)

   b) The slap and pop were obscene threats. Some sat
      Poised like mud grenades, their blunt heads farting. ('Death of a Naturalist')

   c) Our summer made her light escape ('As Imperceptibly as Grief')

   d) The mind-forged manacles I hear: ('London')

   e) And sure as shooting arrows to the heart,
      Astride a dappled mare, legs braced as far apart ('Cozy Apologia')

   f) the wind
      Is ruining their courting-places
      That are still courting-places ('Afternoons')

   g) She walks in beauty, like the night
      Of cloudless climes and starry skies, ('She Walks in Beauty')

   Some of the techniques below are used in more than one of these quotations, and some quotations include more than one technique. State which techniques are being used and explain their effect. You may prefer to write your answers on a separate piece of paper.

   alliteration   archaic language   assonance   caesura   end-stopping   enjambment   metaphor   pathetic fallacy/personification   repetition   rhyming couplet   simile   onomatopoeia

	Technique	Effect
a)		
b)		
c)		
d)		
e)		
f)		
g)		

   [36]

   Total Marks _____ / 36

Poetry

Unseen Poetry

1 Read the poem below and answer the questions that follow. (Use a separate piece of paper if necessary.)

> **Storm in the Black Forest,** D. H. Lawrence
>
> Now it is almost night, from the bronzey soft sky
> jugfull after jugfull of pure white liquid fire, bright white
> tipples over and spills down,
> and is gone
> and gold-bronze flutters bent through the thick upper air.
>
> And as the electric liquid pours out, sometimes
> a still brighter white snake wriggles among it, spilled
> and tumbling wriggling down the sky:
> and then the heavens cackle with uncouth sounds.
>
> And the rain won't come, the rain refuses to come!
>
> This is the electricity that man is supposed to have mastered
> chained, subjugated to his use!
> supposed to!

a) Where and when is it set?

b) Is there a strong regular rhythm or rhyme scheme? If so, what effect does it have? If not, what effect does this have?

c) Give an example of alliteration and explain its effect.

d) Give an example of assonance and explain its effect.

e) Give an example of the use of metaphor and explain its effect.

f) Explain the poet's repeated use of 'and'.

g) What is the significance of the final line 'supposed to!'?

h) What do you think the poem is really about?

i) How does the storm make the poet feel?

j) How does the poem make you feel? [20]

Total Marks _____ / 20

2 Read this poem. (Note that this poem is one stanza.)

The Vixen, John Clare

Among the taller wood with ivy hung,
The old fox plays and dances round her young.
She snuffs and barks if any passes by
And swings her tail and turns prepared to fly.
The horseman hurries by, she bolts to see,
And turns agen, from danger never free.
If any stands she runs among the poles
And barks and snaps and drives them in the holes.
The shepherd sees them and the boy goes by
And gets a stick and progs the hole to try.
They get all still and lie in safety sure,
And out again when everything's secure,
And start and snap at blackbirds bouncing by
To fight and catch the great white butterfly.

Re-read the poem on page 27 and compare the two poems using the chart below.

	'Storm in the Black Forest'	'The Vixen'
Setting (time and place)		In the woods on what seems to be a typical day for the vixen.
What happens in the poem		
Structure		
Rhythm and rhyme		
Vocabulary/register		
Use of sound		
Imagery		
Themes and poet's attitude		

[32]

Total Marks _____ / 32

Post-1914 Prose/Drama

Context and Themes

1 Think about the social, historical and cultural context of the post-1914 text you have studied.

   a) Write a paragraph describing the 'world' of the post-1914 text you have studied. Include information about when and where it is set, the lifestyle of the characters, their attitudes and the attitudes of society in general.

                                                                      [5]

   b) Write a paragraph explaining how this world differs from the world you live in today.

                                                                      [5]

   c) Now think about when the text was written, its genre and form, and its intended audience. Write a paragraph about how these elements are reflected in the text.

                                                                       [5]

2 **a)** In the table below, or on a separate piece of paper, write down some themes that occur in the text you have studied. Try to find four. **[4]**

   b) Now write a sentence or two about each theme, for example:

hypocrisy	In *An Inspector Calls* the Birlings are a respectable middle-class family who seem to embody the moral and social values of the time. The inspector's investigation reveals their failure to live up to these values.

                                                                      [8]

Total Marks _____ / 27

Post-1914 Prose/Drama

Characters

1 Identify the main characters in your novel and draw up and complete a chart for each like the one below:

Name	
Background	
Personality	
Relationships	
Motivation	
Function	

[24]

Language and Structure

2 If you have studied a novel, answer the following questions (a–e).

a) How would you describe the narrator? _____

b) How would you describe the register used by the narrator? _____

c) Have you noticed anything interesting about the way in which any of the characters speak? _____

d) How is your text divided? _____

e) Give an example of the use of figurative language from your text. _____

_____

If you have studied a play, answer these questions (f–j):

f) What, if anything, do we learn from the stage directions? _____

_____

g) Do any of the characters speak directly to the audience? If so, which ones and why? _____

_____

h) Are there any interesting differences between the ways in which characters speak?

_____

i) How is the play divided? _____

j) Give an example of the use of figurative language from your text.

_____

_____ [10]

Total Marks _____ / 34

Nineteenth-Century Prose

Context and Themes

1. Look at these statements about life in the nineteenth century and write a sentence or two saying whether and how each one is reflected in the novel you have studied.

    a) Christianity was part of the fabric of life and writers could assume their readers shared Christian ideas and values.

    Example: **In *Silas Marner*, the moral values are those of Christianity. Virtues such as humility, self-sacrifice and love win out over vices like selfishness, greed and dishonesty.**

    ----

    b) Nineteenth-century Britain was a rich country but many people were extremely poor.

    ----

    c) Nineteenth-century women had far fewer rights than men and a more limited role in society.

    ----

    d) The nineteenth century was a time of discovery, adventure and scientific advances.

    ----

    e) Nineteenth-century writers wrote about both personal feelings and moral responsibility.

    --- [10]

2. a) On a separate piece of paper, write down some themes that occur in the novel you have studied. Try to find five. Here are some examples to get you started:

Pride and Prejudice	social class
Silas Marner	redemption
A Christmas Carol	poverty
Jane Eyre	integrity
War of the Worlds	fear
The Strange Case of Dr Jekyll and Mr Hyde	hypocrisy

[5]

    b) Now write a sentence or two about each of these themes, for example:

In *Pride and Prejudice* awareness of social class can lead to misunderstanding and unhappiness, as well as being a source of humour. [10]

Total Marks _____ / 25

Nineteenth-Century Prose

Characters, Language and Structure

1 Identify the main characters in your novel and draw up a chart for each like the one below:
Try to complete charts for five characters.

Name	
Background	
Personality	
Relationships	
Motivation	
Function	

[25]

2 Below are five quotations from nineteenth-century novels (a–e) and five descriptions of their use of language (v–z). Match each quotation to the appropriate description.

a) It is a truth universally acknowledged that a single man in possession of a good fortune must be in want of a wife.
Pride and Prejudice, Chapter 1

v) The writer uses pathetic fallacy to create a mood.

b) To see the dingy cloud come drooping down, obscuring everything, one might have thought that nature lived hard by and was brewing on a large scale.
A Christmas Carol, stave 1

w) The first-person narrator uses a short, simple sentence for impact.

c) The gold had asked that he should sit weaving longer and longer,
Silas Marner, chapter 14.

x) The author uses irony to amuse the reader, making a statement that is clearly not true.

d) 'This'll tike us rahnd Edgeware?' asked the driver,
War of the Worlds, chapter 16

y) The writer uses personification, making an idea more real by writing as if it were a person.

e) Reader, I married him.
Jane Eyre, Chapter 38

z) The writer uses non-standard English to reflect the origins of the speaker.

[10]

Total Marks _____ / 35

WJEC Eduqas

GCSE ENGLISH LANGUAGE
COMPONENT 1

20th Century Literature Reading and
Creative Prose Writing

PRACTICE PAPER

1 hour 45 minutes

INSTRUCTIONS TO CANDIDATES

Use black ink or black ball-point pen.

Answer **all** questions in Section A.

Select **one** title to use for your writing in Section B.

Write your answers on separate pieces of paper.

You are advised to spend your time as follows:

Section A-about 10 minutes reading
        -about 50 minutes answering the questions

Section B-about 10 minutes planning
        -about 35 minutes writing

INFORMATION FOR CANDIDATES

Section A (Reading): 40 marks

Section B (Writing): 40 marks

The number of marks is given in brackets at the end of each question or part-question.

SECTION A: 40 marks

*Read carefully the passage below. Then answer **all** the questions that follow it.*

This extract is the opening of 'The Invisible Man', a short detective story by G. K. Chesterton, first published in 1911.

In the cool blue twilight of two steep streets in Camden Town, the shop at the corner, a confectioner's,[1] glowed like the butt of a cigar. One should rather say, perhaps, like the butt of a firework, for the light was of many colours and some complexity, broken up by many mirrors and dancing on many gilt and gaily-coloured cakes and sweetmeats. Against this one fiery glass
5 were glued the noses of many gutter-snipes,[2] for the chocolates were all wrapped in those red and gold and green metallic colours which are almost better than chocolate itself; and the huge white wedding-cake in the window was somehow at once remote and satisfying, just as if the whole North Pole were good to eat. Such rainbow provocations could naturally collect the youth of the neighbourhood up to the ages of ten or twelve. But this corner was also attractive to youth at a
10 later stage; and a young man, not less than twenty-four, was staring into the same shop window. To him, also, the shop was of fiery charm, but this attraction was not wholly to be explained by chocolates; which, however, he was far from despising.

    He was a tall, burly, red-haired young man, with a resolute face but a listless manner. He carried under his arm a flat, grey portfolio of black-and-white sketches, which he had sold with more
15 or less success to publishers ever since his uncle (who was an admiral) had disinherited him for Socialism, because of a lecture which he had delivered against that economic theory. His name was John Turnbull Angus.

    Entering at last, he walked through the confectioner's shop to the back room, which was a sort of pastry-cook restaurant, merely raising his hat to the young lady who was serving there. She
20 was a dark, elegant, alert girl in black, with a high colour and very quick, dark eyes; and after the ordinary interval she followed him into the inner room to take his order.

    His order was evidently a usual one. 'I want, please,' he said with precision, 'one halfpenny bun and a small cup of black coffee.' An instant before the girl could turn away he added, 'Also, I want you to marry me.'

25   The young lady of the shop stiffened suddenly, and said: 'Those are jokes I don't allow.'

    The red-haired young man lifted grey eyes of an unexpected gravity

'Really and truly, 'he said, 'it's as serious – as serious as the halfpenny bun. It is expensive, like the bun; one pays for it. It is indigestible, like the bun. It hurts.'

The dark young lady had never taken her dark eyes off him, but seemed to be studying him
30 with almost tragic exactitude. At the end of her scrutiny, she had something like the shadow of a smile, and she sat down in a chair.

'Don't you think,' observed Angus absently, 'that it rather cruel to eat these halfpenny buns? I shall give up these brutal sports when we are married.'

The young lady rose from her chair and walked to the window, evidently in a strong but not
35 unsympathetic cogitation[3]. When at last she swung round again with an air of resolution, she was bewildered to observe that that the young man was carefully laying out on the table various objects from the shop window. They included a pyramid of highly coloured sweets, several plates of sandwiches, and the two decanters containing that mysterious port and sherry which are peculiar to pastry-cooks. In the middle of this neat arrangement he had carefully let down the
40 enormous load of white sugared cake which had been the huge ornament of the window.

'What on earth are you doing?' she asked.

'Duty, my dear Laura,' he began.

'Oh, for the Lord's sake, stop a minute,' she cried, 'and don't talk to me in that way. I mean what is all that?'

45 'A ceremonial meal, Miss Hope,'

'And what is that?' she asked impatiently, pointing to the mountain of sugar.

'The wedding cake, Mrs Angus,' he said.

[1] *confectioner* – a maker or seller of sweets and pastries

[2] *gutter-snipes* – 'street' children

[3] *cogitation* – thinking

Read lines 1–8.

A1 List five things that can be seen through the window of the confectioner's shop. [5]

Read lines 8–12.

A2 How does the writer show how attractive the shop window is to the young man?

You must refer to the language used in the text to support your answer, using relevant subject terminology. [5]

Read lines 13–21.

A3 What impressions do you get of John Turnbull Angus from these lines?

You must refer to the language used in the text to support your answer, using relevant subject terminology. [10]

Read lines 22–34.

A4 How does the writer build the reader's interest in the relationship between Angus and the young lady in these lines?

You should write about:
- what happens in these lines to build the reader's interest
- the writer's use of language and structure
- the effects on the reader

You must refer to the text to support your answer, using relevant subject terminology. [10]

Read from line 35 to the end.

A5 'There is something mysterious and intriguing about the young lady and her reaction to Angus.' How far do you agree with this view?

You should write about:
- your own thoughts and feelings about how Laura is presented here and in the passage as a whole
- how the writer has created these thoughts and feelings.

You must refer to the text to support your answer. [10]

SECTION B: 40 marks

*In this section you will be assessed for the quality of your **creative prose writing** skills.*

24 marks are awarded for communication and organisation. 16 marks are awarded for vocabulary, sentence structure, spelling and punctuation.

You should aim to write about 450-600 words.

Choose one of the following titles for your writing: [40]

Either,

     (a) Looking through the Window.

Or,

     (b) A Big Decision.

Or,

     (c) Write a story which begins:

     I never expected much to happen while I was serving coffee to strangers.

Or,

     (d) Write about a person who made a big impression on you.

GCSE ENGLISH LANGUAGE

COMPONENT 2

19th and 21st Century Non-fiction Reading and
Transactional / Persuasive Writing

PRACTICE PAPER

2 hours

INSTRUCTIONS TO CANDIDATES

Use black ink or black ball-point pen.

Answer **all** questions in Sections A and B

Write your answers on separate pieces of paper.

You are advised to spend your time as follows:

Section A-about 10 minutes reading

        -about 50 minutes answering the questions

Section B-spend 30 minutes on each question

        -about 5 minutes planning

        -about 25 minutes writing

INFORMATION FOR CANDIDATES

Section A (Reading): 40 marks

Section B (Writing): 40 marks

The number of marks is given in brackets at the end of each question or part-question.

GCSE English Workbook

SECTION A: 40 marks

*Answer **all** the following questions.*

The extract below is a newspaper article by Alfie Witherspoon.

SAVE OUR LIBRARY

Local writer joins the fight against closure

By our Arts and Education Correspondent, Alfie Witherspoon

The campaign to save King's Park Library from closure has the backing of an array of local talent. Children's writer Mandy Frobisher says that without the library she would never have become a writer.

'I can't tell you how much that library meant to me,' she told me. 'It gave me a refuge, a place to do my homework, access to centuries of learning and a lifelong love of literature. It made me who I am.
5   Why should today's children be deprived of the opportunities which our generation took for granted?'

Actor Steve Gomez agrees wholeheartedly. 'When I was growing up, the library was the centre of our community. People from all walks of life and all ages used it. They still do. If it closes, there'll be a black hole at the heart of King's Park.' Steve may not mean this literally, but other locals are concerned about what will happen to the building itself, a purpose-built, generously proportioned,
10   roomy building beautifully decorated in the style of the Edwardian Arts and Crafts movement.

Campaigners have high hopes that the backing of Mary and Steve, and other well-known local figures, will help to publicize their campaign and maybe even persuade the Mayor and council to change their minds.

However, a spokesperson for the council claims that the facts simply don't justify keeping the
15   library open. Statistics show that there are now fewer than 300 regular borrowers, almost all of them pensioners, and that number is falling all the time. Figures for people using the references facilities are equally depressing, with only a handful of knowledge-seekers using the facilities each day.

Nevertheless, campaign leader Councillor Laurel Tompkins says she will continue to fight the closure 'every inch of the way'. According to her, the savings to be made by shutting King's Park
20   and five other local libraries are 'a drop in the ocean'. She acknowledges the government has made cuts in its funding – and that King's Park isn't the thriving, populous area it once was – but is convinced that it is not worth devastating the community for a comparatively small saving. 'And when new research is showing that one in three children in the UK does not own a book,' she adds, 'how can the Mayor deprive our kids of the chance of borrowing one and being turned on to
25   reading for life?'

The following text is a letter to The Times, written in 1891, about a vote on the issues of public libraries in the London district of Marylebone. Under the Public Libraries Act, people had to vote in favour of public libraries before they could be built by a local council. This letter is from representatives of a group that was running free libraries without public funding.

PUBLIC LIBRARIES IN MARYLEBONE: TO THE EDITOR OF *THE TIMES*

Sir,– May we be allowed, through your columns, to appeal to the ratepayers[1] of Marylebone to record their votes at the end of the present week in favour of the adoption of the Public Libraries Acts, and thus secure for this large and wealthy parish the inestimable social advantages of good libraries, free to all classes, in every district?

5   We do not make this appeal in order to expatiate upon these advantages, because, with free libraries springing up in all directions, they are generally admitted. We would rather remind Marylebone of the work which our voluntary association has accomplished during the last three years – a work which must, in all probability, be brought to an end within the next year or so, unless the financial burden of maintaining the existing voluntary libraries be transferred from our association to the ratepayers at large.

   The history of the Marylebone Free Library movement is briefly this:– An effort was made in 1887 to obtain
10   sufficient funds, £20,000, to erect a handsome central library, which should not only be a permanent Jubilee[2] memorial, but also serve as a stimulus to the inhabitants of Marylebone to adopt the Public Libraries Acts. The movement failed, only about £7,000 being promised, and an appeal to the ratepayers the following year failed also, not so much from opposition as from apathy on the part of the inhabitants. Our association, in no wise daunted, decided to establish small local reading rooms and libraries in two of the most populous parts of the
15   parish, in the hope that by these object-lessons demonstration amounting to proof would be given both of a great social need and a successful means of meeting it. We have not been mistaken in our calculations. The library in Lisson-grove, opened in 1889, has been an extraordinary success. The space is limited, and accommodation plain and insufficient, but notwithstanding these drawbacks no less than 219,000 persons of all sorts and conditions have used the news and reading room and the reference and lending libraries during the past year. A carefully
20   selected library of 4,000 volumes has attracted 1,200 borrowers, whilst the demand increases daily. Our second library in Mortimer-street, nearly opposite the Middlesex Hospital, was only opened nine months ago and is on a smaller scale. Its success, however, is proportionately greater. Funds, and funds only, are required to enable the association to multiply these useful institutions. One library is £300 in debt, and the funds of the second are running low. Unfortunately, many of our actual and also many of our would-be subscribers feel that the very
25   success of our movement relieves them of individual responsibility. That which exists, they say, for the good of all should be paid for by all, more especially when the maximum amount imposed upon each ratepayer by the 1d. rate[3] is so trifling. During the past few years no less than 28 metropolitan and suburban districts, some poor, some rich, have adopted the Public Libraries Acts. Others are about to follow, and our association hopes that Marylebone will be of the number. Much want of knowledge and indifference still exist on the subject of free
30   libraries, and we therefore appeal to you to give publicity to our case, and thus contribute to success at the poll.

We beg, Sir, to remain yours obediently,

JOHN R. HOLLOND Chairman

FRANK DEBENHAM Treasurer

Marylebone Public Libraries Association, 18 Baker-street. March 4.

[1] *ratepayers* – people who pay 'rates' or local taxes, the equivalent of Council Tax today
[2] *Jubilee* – the golden jubilee of Queen Victoria had taken place in 1887
[3] *1d. rate* – a one-penny tax; local councils could increase rates by up to a penny per pound for libraries and museums.

Read the newspaper article by Alfie Witherspoon.

A1 (a) What audience does Mandy Frobisher write for? [1]

(b) How many people regularly borrow books from the library? [1]

(c) How many libraries is the Council proposing to close? [1]

A2 What do you think of the campaign to save King's Park Library as described in the article?

You should comment on:
- what both campaigners and their opponents say
- how they say it

You must refer to the text to support your comments. [10]

To answer the following questions you will need to read the letter to *The Times*.

A3 (a) What are the writers trying to persuade readers of the newspaper to do? [2]

(b) What do they mean by saying the advantages of libraries are 'generally admitted'? [1]

A4 How do the writers of the letter try to persuade people to support their point of view?

You should comment on:
- what they say to influence readers
- their use of language and tone
- the way they present their argument. [10]

To answer the following questions you will need to use both texts.

A5 What are the main differences between King's Park Library now and the two Marylebone libraries in 1891? [4]

A6 Both the texts are about public libraries. Compare the following:
- the writers' attitudes to libraries
- how they put across these attitudes.

You must use the texts to support your comments and make clear which text you are referring to. [10]

SECTION B: 40 marks

*Answer questions B1 **and** B2.*
In this section you will assessed for the quality of your writing skills.

For each question, 12 marks are awarded for communication and organisation; 8 marks are awarded for vocabulary, sentence structure, spelling and punctuation.

Think about the purpose and audience of your writing.

You should aim to write about 300-400 words for each task.

B1 The council has announced that it is planning to close your local library.

Write a letter to the local newspaper giving your views. [20]

B2 Your school supports a different charity each term. Your form has chosen this term's charity and has asked you to write an article for the school magazine or website about your plans to raise money.

Write your article.

You could include:

- details of your chosen charity and an explanation of why you have chosen it and why others should support it
- details of your plans for money-raising activities. [20]

WJEC Eduqas

GCSE ENGLISH LITERATURE
COMPONENT 1

Shakespeare and Poetry

PRACTICE PAPER

2 hours

Section A

Question

1   *Macbeth*
2   *Romeo and Juliet*
3   *Henry V*
4   *The Merchant of Venice*
5   *Much Ado About Nothing*
6   *Othello*

Section B

Question

7   Poetry

INSTRUCTIONS TO CANDIDATES

Answer two questions: one from Section A (questions 1-6) **and** Section B (question 7).

INFORMATION FOR CANDIDATES

Each section carries 40 marks.

You are advised to spend your time as follows:

Section A - about one hour

Section B - about one hour

The number of marks is given in brackets at the end of each question or part-question.

5 marks are given for accuracy in spelling, punctuation and the use of vocabulary and sentence structures in Section A, question part (b).

Practice Exam Papers

SECTION A: Shakespeare

Answer on one text only.

1. **Macbeth**

   *Answer **both** part (a) **and** part (b).*

   You are advised to spend about 20 minutes on part (a) and about 40 minutes on part (b).

   (a) Read the extract below.

   Look at how Macbeth speaks and behaves here. What does it tell the audience about his state of mind at this point in the play? Refer closely to details from the extract to support your answer. **[15]**

MACBETH	I have almost forgot the taste of fears.
	The time has been my senses would have cooled
	To hear the night-shriek, and my fell of hair
	Would at a dismal treatise rise and stir
	As life were in't. I have supped full with horrors.
	Direness, familiar to my slaughterous thoughts,
	Cannot once start me.
Enter Seyton	
	Wherefore was that cry?
SEYTON	The Queen, my lord, is dead.
MACBETH	She should have died hereafter.
	There would have been a time for such a word.
	Tomorrow, and tomorrow, and tomorrow
	Creeps in this petty pace from day to day
	To the last syllable of recorded time,
	And all our yesterdays have lighted fools
	The way to dusty death. Out, out, brief candle.
	Life's but a walking shadow, a poor player
	That struts and frets his hour upon the stage,
	And then is heard no more. It is a tale
	Told by an idiot, full of sound and fury,
	Signifying nothing.

   ***(b)** Write about how Shakespeare presents the relationship between Macbeth and Lady Macbeth at different points in the play. **[25]**

   5 of this question's marks are allocated for accuracy in spelling, punctuation and the use of vocabulary and sentence structures.

2. *Romeo and Juliet*

    Answer **both** part (a) **and** part (b).

    You are advised to spend about 20 minutes on part (a) and about 40 minutes on part (b).

    (a) Read the extract below.

    Look at how Romeo and Juliet speak and behave here. What does it tell the audience about their relationship at this point in the play? Refer closely to details from the extract to support your answer.

    [15]

JULIET	Wilt thou be gone? It is not yet near day.
	It was the nightingale, and not the lark,
	That pierced the fear-full hollow of thine ear.
	Nightly she sings on yon pomegranate tree.
	Believe me, love, it was the nightingale.
ROMEO	It was the lark, the herald of the morn,
	No nightingale. Look, love, what envious streaks
	Do lace the severing clouds in yonder east.
	Night's candles are burnt out, and jocund day
	Stands tiptoe on the misty mountain tops.
	I must be gone and live, or stay and die.
JULIET	Yon light is not daylight; I know it, I.
	It is some meteor that the sun exhaled
	To be to thee this night a torchbearer
	And light thee on thy way to Mantua.
	Therefore stay yet. Thou need'st not be gone.

    *(b) Write about how Shakespeare presents Romeo's feelings towards Juliet in the play as a whole.

    [25]

    *5 of this question's marks are allocated for accuracy in spelling, punctuation and the use of vocabulary and sentence structures.

3. *Henry V*

    *Answer **both** part (a) **and** part (b).*

    You are advised to spend about 20 minutes on part (a) and about 40 minutes on part (b).

    (a) Read the extract below.

    > Look at how the characters speak and behave here. How would an audience respond to this part of the play? Refer closely to details from the extract to support your answer. **[15]**

BARDOLPH	On,on,on,on,on! To the breach, to the breach!.
NIM	Pray thee corporal, stay. The knocks are too hot, and for mine own part, I have not a case of lives. The honour of it is too hot, that is the very plainsong of it.

PISTOL	'The plainsong' is most just, for humours do abound. Knocks
	Go and come God's vassals drop and die,
	[*sings*]And sword and shield
	    In bloody field
	    Doth win immortal fame.

BOY	Would I were in London. I would give all my fame for a pot of ale, and safety.
PISTOL	[*sings*] And I If wishes would prevail with me My purpose should not fail with me But thither would I hie.
BOY	[*sings*]As duly But not as truly As bird doth sing on bough. [*Enter Captain Fluellen and beats them in*]
FLUELLEN	God's plud! Up to the breaches, you dogs! Avaunt you cullions!
PISTOL	Be merciful, great duke, to men of mould. Abate thy rage, abate thy manly rage, Abate thy rage, great duke. Good bawcock, bate Thy rage. Use lenity, sweet chuck.

NIM	These be good humours!
	    [*Fluellen begins to beat Nim*]
	Your honour runs bad humours.
	    Exeunt all but the boy

BOY	As young as I am, I have observed these three swashers. I am boy to them all three, but all they three, though they should serve me, could not be man to me, for indeed three such antucs do not amount to a man,

(b) Write about how an audience might react to King Henry's speeches at different points in the play.
[25]

> *5 of this question's marks are allocated for accuracy in spelling, punctuation and the use of vocabulary and sentence structures.*

4. *The Merchant of Venice*

*Answer **both** part (a) **and** part (b).*

You are advised to spend about 20 minutes on part (a) and about 40 minutes on part (b).

(a) Read the extract below.

Look at how Antonio and Shylock speak and behave here. How does Shakespeare present Shylock as an outsider at this point in the play? Refer closely to details from the extract to support your answer.

[15]

SHYLOCK	Jailer, look to him. Tell me not of mercy.
	This is the fool that lent the money gratis.
	Jailer, look to him.
ANTONIO	Hear me yet, good Shylock.
SHYLOCK	I'll have my bond. Speak not against my bond.
	I have sworn an oath that I will have my bond.
	Thou called'st me a dog before thou hadst a cause,
	But since I am a dog, beware my fangs.
	The Duke shall grant me justice. I do wonder,
	Thou naughty jailer, that thou art so fond
	To come abroad with him at his request.
ANTONIO	I pray thee hear me speak.
SHYLOCK	I'll have my bond. I will not hear thee speak.
	I'll have my bond, and therefore speak not me more.
	I'll not be made a soft and dull-eyed fool
	To shake the head, relent, and sigh, and yield
	To Christian intercessors. Follow not.
	I'll have no speaking. I will have my bond.

*(b)** How does Shakespeare explore ideas about justice and mercy in the play as a whole?

[25]

5 of this question's marks are allocated for accuracy in spelling, punctuation and the use of vocabulary and sentence structures.

5. *Much Ado About Nothing*

   *Answer **both** part (a) **and** part (b).*

   You are advised to spend about 20 minutes on part (a) and about 40 minutes on part (b).

   (a) Read the extract below.

   Look at how the characters speak and behave here. What does it tell the audience about the relationship between Beatrice and Benedick at this point in the play? Refer closely to details from the extract to support your answer.   **[15]**

LEONATO	Faith, niece, you tax Signor Benedick too much. But he'll be meet with you, I doubt it not.
MESSENGER	He hath done good service, lady, in these wars.
BEATRICE	You had musty victual, and he hath holp to eat it. He is a very valiant trencherman, he hath an excellent stomach.
MESSENGER	And a good soldier too, lady.
BEATRICE	And a good soldier to a lady, but what is he to a lord?
MESSENGER	A lord to a lord, a man to a man, stuffed with all honourable virtues.
BEATRICE	It is so, indeed. He is no less than a stuffed man. But for the stuffing – well, we are all mortal.
LEONATO	You must not, sir, mistake my niece. There is a kind of merry war betwixt Signor Benedick and her. They never meet but there's a skirmish of wit between them.

   *(b) Write about how Shakespeare presents ideas about honour in the play as a whole.   **[25]**

   *5 of this question's marks are allocated for accuracy in spelling, punctuation and the use of vocabulary and sentence structures.

6. *Othello*

   Answer **both** part (a) **and** part (b).

   You are advised to spend about 20 minutes on part (a) and about 40 minutes on part (b).

   (a) Read the extract below.

   Look at how Othello speaks and behaves here. How would an audience respond to this part of the play? Refer closely to details from the extract to support your answer. **[15]**

OTHELLO	Soft you, a word or two before you go.
	I have done the state some service and they know't;
	No more of that: I pray you in your letters,
	When you shall these unlucky deeds relate,
	Speak of them as they are; nothing extenuate,
	Nor set down aught in malice; then must you speak
	Of one that loved not wisely but too well:
	Of one not easily jealous, but being wrought,
	Perplexed in the extreme; of one whose hand,
	Like the base Indian, threw a pearl away,
	Richer than all his tribe; of one whose subdued eyes,
	Albeit unused to the melting mood.
	Drops tears as fast as the Arabian trees
	Their medicinal gum; set you down this,
	And say besides, that in Aleppo once,
	Where a malignant and turbaned Turk
	Beat a Venetian, and traduced the state,
	I took him by the throat the circumcised dog,
	And smote him thus.
	He stabs himself
LODOVICO	O bloody prevail!
GRATIANO	All that's spoke is marred.
OTHELLO	I kissed thee ere I killed thee, no way but this,
	Killing myself, to die upon a kiss.

   *(b) Write about how an audience might react to the character of Iago at different points in the play.

   [25]

   *5 of this question's marks are allocated for accuracy in spelling, punctuation and the use of vocabulary and sentence structures.

Practice Exam Papers

SECTION B: Poetry

7. Answer **both** part (a) **and** part (b).

You are advised to spend about 20 minutes on part (a) and about 40 minutes on part (b).

(a) Read the poem *London* by William Blake. In this poem Blake writes about human suffering. Write about the ways in which he presents human suffering in this poem.   **[15]**

(b) Choose **one** other poem from the anthology in which the poet also writes about suffering.

Compare the presentation of suffering in your chosen poem to the presentation of suffering in *London*.   **[25]**

In your answer to part (b) you should compare:
- the content and structure of poems – what they are about and how they are organised;
- how the writers create effects, using appropriate terminology where relevant;
- the contexts of the poems and how these might have influenced the ideas in them.

London **by William Blake**

I wander through each chartered street,
Near where the chartered Thames does flow,
And mark in every face I meet
Marks of weakness, marks of woe.

In every cry of every man,
In every infant's cry of fear,
In every voice, in every ban,
The mind-forged manacles I hear:

How the chimney-sweeper's cry
Every black'ning church appals
And the hapless soldier's sigh
Runs in blood down palace walls.

But most through midnight streets I hear
How the youthful harlot's curse
Blasts the new-born infant's tear,
And blights with plague the marriage hearse.

WJEC Eduqas

GCSE ENGLISH LITERATURE
COMPONENT 2

Post-1914 Prose/Drama, 19th Century Prose and Unseen Poetry

PRACTICE PAPER

2 hours and 30 minutes

Section A
Questions
1   *An Inspector Calls*
2   *Blood Brothers*
3   *The History Boys*
4   *The Curious Incident of the Dog in the Night-Time*
5   *A Taste of Honey*
6   *Lord of the Flies*
7   *Never Let Me Go*
8   *Anita and Me*
9   *The Woman in Black*
10 *Oranges are not the Only Fruit*

Section B
Questions
11 *The Strange Case of Dr Jekyll and Mr Hyde*
12 *A Christmas Carol*
13 *Jane Eyre*
14 *Pride and Prejudice*
15 *Silas Marner*
16 *War of the Worlds*

Section C
Question
17 *Unseen Poetry*

Instructions to Candidates

Answer **one** question in Section A (questions 1-10), **one** question in Section B (questions 11-16) **and** Section C (question 17).

Information for Candidates

Each section carries 40 marks.

You are advised to spend your time as follows:
Section A - about 45 minutes
Section B - about 45 minutes
Section C - about one hour

The number of marks is given in brackets at the end of each question or part-question.
5 marks are allocated for accuracy in spelling, punctuation and the use of vocabulary and sentence structures in Section A.

SECTION A: Post-1914 Prose/Drama

Answer one question only from this section.

1. *An Inspector Calls*

You are advised to spend about 45 minutes on this question.

You should use the extract referred to below and your knowledge of the whole text to answer the question.

Write about the significance of Eva Smith and how she is presented in *An Inspector Calls*.

In your response you should:
- refer to the extract and the play as a whole
- show your understanding of the characters and events in the play. [40]

5 of this question's marks are given for accuracy in spelling, punctuation, sentence structure and vocabulary

---

Re-read Act 1 from

INSPECTOR: I'd like some information, if you don't mind, Mr Birling.

to

INSPECTOR: It's the way I like to work. One person and one line of inquiry at a time. Otherwise, there's a muddle.

---

2. *Blood Brothers*

You are advised to spend about 45 minutes on this question.

You should use the extract referred to below and your knowledge of the whole text to answer the question.

Write about how Russell uses Mickey and Edward to explore ideas about social class in *Blood Brothers*.

In your response you should:
- refer to the extract and the play as a whole
- show your understanding of the characters and events in the play. [40]

5 of this question's marks are given for accuracy in spelling, punctuation, sentence structure and vocabulary

---

Re-read Act 1 from

MICKEY (off): Does Eddie live here?

to

MRS LYONS: Because, because you're not the same as him. You're not, do you understand?

---

3. *The History Boys*

You are advised to spend about 45 minutes on this question.

You should use the extract referred to below and your knowledge of the whole text to answer the question.

Write about how Bennett presents different attitudes to history in *The History Boys*.

In your response you should:
- refer to the extract and the play as a whole
- show your understanding of the characters and events in the play. **[40]**

5 of this question's marks are given for accuracy in spelling, punctuation, sentence structure and vocabulary

> **Re-read Act 2 from**
>
> *IRWIN: If you want to learn about Stalin study Henry VIII.*
>
> **to**
>
> *IRWIN: God is dead. Shit lives.*

4. *The Curious Incident of the Dog in the Night-Time*

You are advised to spend about 45 minutes on this question.

You should use the extract referred to below and your knowledge of the whole text to answer the question.

Write about how Stephens presents the character of Judy as a mother in *The Curious Incident of the Dog in the Night-Time*.

In your response you should:
- refer to the extract and the play as a whole
- show your understanding of the characters and events in the play. **[40]**

5 of this question's marks are given for accuracy in spelling, punctuation, sentence structure and vocabulary

> **Re-read Act 2 from**
>
> *JUDY: Dear Christopher. I said that I wanted to explain to you why I went away when I had time to do it properly.*
>
> **to**
>
> *JUDY: And then I had to walk you all the way home, which took hours because I knew you wouldn't go on the bus again.*

5. *A Taste of Honey*

You are advised to spend about 45 minutes on this question.

You should use the extract referred to below and your knowledge of the whole text to answer the question.

Write about the character of Jo and how she is presented in *A Taste of Honey*.

In your response you should:
- refer to the extract and the play as a whole
- show your understanding of the characters and events in the play. **[40]**

5 of this question's marks are given for accuracy in spelling, punctuation, sentence structure and vocabulary

---

Re-read Act 1 from

Jo: Won't be long now. Who lives here besides us, Helen. Any young people?

to

Jo: It's nice to see a few flowers, isn't it?

---

6. *Lord of the Flies*

You are advised to spend about 45 minutes on this question.

You should use the extract referred to below and your knowledge of the whole text to answer the question.

How does Golding present ideas about the breakdown of civilisation in *Lord of the Flies*?

In your response you should:
- refer to the extract and the novel as a whole
- show your understanding of the characters and events in the novel. **[40]**

5 of this question's marks are given for accuracy in spelling, punctuation, sentence structure and vocabulary

---

Re-read Chapter 8 from

The forest near them burst into uproar.

to

Then the three of them turned and trotted away.

---

7. *Never Let Me Go*

You are advised to spend about 45 minutes on this question.

You should use the extract referred to below and your knowledge of the whole text to answer the question.

Write about the guardians and how they are presented in *Never Let Me Go.*

In your response you should:
- refer to the extract and the novel as a whole
- show your understanding of the characters and events in the novel. **[40]**

5 of this question's marks are given for accuracy in spelling, punctuation, sentence structure and vocabulary

---

Re-read Chapter 3 from

> *Tommy had heard all this before, but there was something about Miss Lucy's manner that made him keep listening hard.*

to

> *'Anyway, when she said all this, she was shaking.'*

---

8. *Anita and Me*

You are advised to spend about 45 minutes on this question.

You should use the extract referred to below and your knowledge of the whole text to answer the question.

Write about how racism is presented in *Anita and Me.*

In your response you should:
- refer to the extract and the novel as a whole
- show your understanding of the characters and events in the novel. **[40]**

5 of this question's marks are given for accuracy in spelling, punctuation, sentence structure and vocabulary

---

Re-read Chapter 5 from

> *I had expected aggression, some name calling, the kind of hissed comments I occasionally endured from the young lads on the council estate near my school, the school where mama taught.*

to

> *Mama said, 'Wipe your nose,' and handed me a tissue and we went inside.*

---

9. *The Woman in Black*

   You are advised to spend about 45 minutes on this question.

   You should use the extract referred to below and your knowledge of the whole text to answer the question.

   How does Hill write about supernatural events in *The Woman in Black*?

   In your response you should:
   - refer to the extract and the novel as a whole
   - show your understanding of the characters and events in the novel.   **[40]**

   5 of this question's marks are given for accuracy in spelling, punctuation, sentence structure and vocabulary

   ---

   Re-read 'The Funeral of Mrs Drablow' from

   > *At last he said in a low voice, 'I did not see a young woman,'*

   to

   > *'No!' He almost shrieked.*

   ---

10. *Oranges are not the Only Fruit*

    You are advised to spend about 45 minutes on this question.

    You should use the extract referred to below and your knowledge of the whole text to answer the question.

    How does Winterson present ideas about identity and belonging in *Oranges are not the Only Fruit*?

    In your response you should:
    - refer to the extract and the novel as a whole
    - show your understanding of the characters and events in the novel.   **[40]**

    5 of this question's marks are given for accuracy in spelling, punctuation, sentence structure and vocabulary

    ---

    Re-read 'Joshua' from

    > *The Awful Occasion was the time my natural mother had come to claim me back.*

    to

    > *She never spoke of what had happened and neither did I.*

SECTION B: 19th-Century Prose

*Answer **one** question only from this section.*

11. *The Strange Case of Dr Jekyll and Mr Hyde*

    You are advised to spend about 45 minutes on this question.

    You should use the extract referred to below and your knowledge of the whole novel to answer this question.

    Write about how Stevenson uses Jekyll's transformation to explore ideas about good and evil in the novel.

    In your response you should:
    - refer to the extract and the novel as a whole;
    - show your understanding of characters and events in the novel;
    - refer to the contexts of the novel. [40]

    Re-read Chapter 8 ('The Last Night') from

    'That's it!' said Poole. 'It was this way. I came suddenly into the theatre from the garden. It seems he had slipped out to look for this drug or whatever it is; for the cabinet door was open, and there he was at the far end of the room digging among the crates...'

    to

    '...No, sir, that thing in the mask was never Doctor Jekyll – God knows what it was but it was never Doctor Jekyll; and it is the belief of my heart that there was murder done.'

12. *A Christmas Carol*

You are advised to spend about 45 minutes on this question.

You should use the extract referred to below and your knowledge of the whole novel to answer this question.

How does Dickens write about social problems in the novel?

In your response you should:
* refer to the extract and the novel as a whole;
* show your understanding of characters and events in the novel;
* refer to the contexts of the novel.

[40]

Re-read Stave (Chapter) 3 from

'Forgive me if I am not justified in what I ask,' said Scrooge, looking intently at the Spirit's robe, *'but I see something strange, and not belonging to yourself, protruding from your skirts. Is it a foot or a claw?'*

to

Are there no prisons?' said the Spirit, turning on him for the last time with his own words. *'Are there no workhouses?'*

---

13. *Jane Eyre*

You are advised to spend about 45 minutes on this question.

You should use the extract referred to below and your knowledge of the whole novel to answer this question.

Write about how Brontë presents the character of Mr Rochester and Jane's changing feelings towards him.

In your response you should:
- refer to the extract and the novel as a whole;
- show your understanding of characters and events in the novel;
- refer to the contexts of the novel. [40]

Re-read Chapter 15 from

And was Mr Rochester now ugly in my eyes?

to

Suppose he should be absent spring, summer, and autumn: how joyless sunshine and fine days will seem!

14. *Pride and Prejudice*

You are advised to spend about 45 minutes on this question.

You should use the extract referred to below and your knowledge of the whole novel to answer this question.

How does Austen write about attitudes to marriage in the novel?

In your response you should:
- refer to the extract and the novel as a whole;
- show your understanding of characters and events in the novel;
- refer to the contexts of the novel.

[40]

Re-read Chapter 20 from

'An unhappy alternative is before you, Elizabeth. From this day you must be a stranger to one of your parents. – Your mother will never see you again if you do not marry Mr Collins, and I will never see you again if you do.'

to

A*'But I tell you what, Miss Lizzy, if you take it into your head to go on refusing every offer of marriage in this way, you will never get a husband at all – and I am sure I do not know who is to aintain you when your father is dead.'*

---

15. *Silas Marner*

You are advised to spend about 45 minutes on this question.

You should use the extract referred to below and your knowledge of the whole novel to answer this question.

Write about Silas's relationship with Eppie and how it is presented in the novel.

In your response you should:
- refer to the extract and the novel as a whole;
- show your understanding of characters and events in the novel;
- refer to the contexts of the novel. **[40]**

Re-read Chapter 12 from

When Marner's sensibility returned, he continued the action which had been arrested, and closed his door…

to

-that there was a human body, with the head sunk low into the furze, and half-covered with the shaken snow.

---

16. *War of the Worlds*

You are advised to spend about 45 minutes on this question.

You should use the extract referred to below and your knowledge of the whole novel to answer this question.

Write about how Wells presents the reactions of different characters to the invasion at different points in the novel.

In your response you should:
- refer to the extract and the novel as a whole;
- show your understanding of characters and events in the novel;
- refer to the contexts of the novel. [40]

Re-read Book 1, Chapter 13 from

I do not clearly remember the arrival of the curate…

to

'Killed!' he said, staring about him. 'How can God's ministers be killed?'

SECTION C: Unseen Poetry

17. Answer **both** part (a) **and** part (b).

You are advised to spend about 20 minutes on part (a) and about 40 minutes on part (b).

Read the two poems, *Death the Leveller* by James Shirley and *Requiem* by Robert Louis Stevenson. In both these poems the poets write about their feeling about death.

(a) Write about *Death the Leveller* and its effect on you.   **[15]**

You may wish to consider:
- what the poem is about and how it is organised;
- the ideas the poet may have wanted us to think about;
- the poet's choice of words, phrases and images and the effects they create;
- how you respond to the poem.

Death the Leveller, James Shirley

The glories of our blood and state
    Are shadows, not substantial things;
There is no armour against Fate;
    Death lays his icy hand on kings:
5   Sceptre and Crown
        Must tumble down,
And in the dust be equal made
    With the poor crookèd scythe and spade.

Some men with swords may reap the field,
10   And plant fresh laurels where they kill:
But their strong nerves at last must yield;
    They tame but one another still:
        Early or late
        They stoop to fate,
15 And must give up their murmuring breath
    When they, pale captives, creep to death.

The garlands wither on your brow,
    Then boast no more your mighty deeds!
Upon Death's purple altar now
20   See where the victor-victim bleeds.
        Your heads must come
        To the cold tomb:
Only the actions of the just
    Smell sweet and blossom in their dust.

(b) Now compare *Death the Leveller* and *Requiem*.   [25]

You should compare:

- what the poems are about and how they are organised;
- the ideas the poets may have wanted us to think about;
- the poets' choice of words, phrases and images and the effects they create;
- how you respond to the poems.

Requiem, Robert Louis Stevenson

Under the wide and starry sky,
Dig the grave and let me lie.
Glad did I live and gladly die,
And I laid me down with a will.

5   This be the verse you gave for me:
Here he lies where he longed to be;
Home is the sailor, home from the sea,
And the hunter home from the hill.

Answers

Key Technical Skills: Writing – pages 4–8

Page 4: Spelling

1. a) tomatoes   b) birthdays
   c) soliloquies   d) families
   e) parentheses   **[maximum 5]**
2. a) **You're** not going out like that. I asked **your** sister to bring it.
   b) **There** are twenty people in the class. They have all done **their** homework but **they're** not sitting in the right places.
   c) Turn it off or it will **wear** out. We have no idea **where** it is but **we're** going anyway.
   d) I **passed** him in the street an hour ago. He walked right **past** me as if I wasn't there.
   e) There were only **two** exams **to** sit but that was one **too** many.
   f) If you don't go to the **practice** you'll be left out of the team. If you want to improve you will have to **practise** every day.
        [1] for each correct answer up to a maximum of **[15]**
3. Last **night** I went to the cinema with my friend Bob and his **father**, Michael. The whole evening was not very **successful**. The cinema was very **crowded** and we had to sit **separately**. Then, it turned out the film was in a **foreign language** and no-one could understand it. I think it was about the **environment**. Afterwards, Michael took us to a **restaurant where** we had pizzas.
        [1] for each correct answer up to a maximum of **[10]**

Page 5: Punctuation

1. *Great Expectations,* **[1]** one of the best-known novels by Charles Dickens, **[1]** is the story of Pip, **[1]** a boy who grows up in the marshes of Kent. At **[1]** the beginning of the story he meets an escaped convict in the churchyard where his parents are buried. **[1]**   **[maximum 5]**
2. At about ten o'clock **[1]**, we went to Romio's **[1]** for pizzas. I'm **[1]** not sure what Bob's **[1]** pizza topping was but I had ham and pineapple. I wish I hadn't **[1]** because later on I was sick in Michael's **[1]** car. It's **[1]** brand new and I thought he'd **[1]** be angry but he wasn't **[1]**. We're **[1]** not going there again.   **[maximum 10]**
3. a) The cat slept quietly on the mat; the dog slept noisily on the step. b) Who was that masked man? Nobody knows. c) I don't believe it! That's the first answer I've got. d) Annie deserved the prize: she was the best baker by far. e) Jane and Elizabeth (the two oldest Bennet sisters) get married at the end.
        [1] for each correct answer up to a maximum of **[5]**

Page 6: Sentence Structure

1. a) complex   b) minor   c) simple
   d) compound   e) simple
        [maximum of 5]
2. a) I bought Anna a bunch of flowers **because** it was her birthday. **[1]**
   b) He did not finish the race **although** they gave him a certificate. **[1]**
   a) and b) could be written with the conjunctions at the beginning of the sentence, but you would then need to add a comma after the first clause.
   c) I kept going **until** I reached the finishing line. **[1]**

3. Joey, who was the oldest cat in the street, never left the garden. **[1]**
4. Walking down the street, I realised I had forgotten my phone. **[1]**

Page 7: Text Structure and Organisation

1. a) 3
   b) 5
   c) 2
   d) 4
   e) 1   **[maximum 5]**
2. a) When
   b) In spite of
   c) subsequently
   d) however
   e) Nevertheless   **[maximum 5]**

Page 8: Standard English and Grammar

1. a) are   b) are   c) were   d) did
   e) has been   f) have done   g) were...had done
        [maximum 7]
2. a) pleaded   b) few   c) got
        [maximum 3]
3. Jo: Hello. How are you? **[1]**
   Arthur: Well. Very well, thank you. **[1]**
   Jo: Do you want (*or* would you like) a drink? **[1]**
   Arthur: May I have two coffees, please? **[1]**
   Jo: Of course. Where are you sitting? **[1]**
4. I was **standing** in the street when Frankie **came** over. **[1]** I gave him a smile and opened **my mouth** to speak. **[1]** I was **going to** ask him how he **did** in **maths** (*or* **mathematics**). **[1]** I **did not say anything.** **[1]** As soon as I **saw** him I knew he **had done well.** **[1]**

Key Technical Skills: Reading – pages 9–16

Page 9: Identifying Information and Ideas 1

1. a, c   **[maximum 2]**
2. **Any five from**: He was very nice looking. He had a fresh-coloured face. He was clean shaven. He had white hair. He wore odd-shaped collars. He wore a top hat.   **[maximum 5]**

Page 10: Identifying Information and Ideas 2

1. a) Year 10   b) No
   c) Solicitor   d) Answered the telephone
   e) No   **[maximum 5]**

Page 11: Synthesis and Summary

1. a) Trees stand behind the shed. **[1]** b) Charlotte Green ate Lydia's chocolate. **[1]** c) Tell me who did it. **[1]**
2. b, c, f, g, h   **[maximum 5]**
3. The summary below is a suggestion only. You should have included details of where and when it happened, and a description of the men.
        [1] for each point up to a maximum of **[12]**.

   At nine o'clock on Monday I was in Arbuckle Lane. As I passed number eighteen, I heard a noise. There were two men on the step. One was breaking the glass in the door with something in his hand. I shouted and they turned. One was about six foot, with a grey beard. The other was stocky with curly black hair. The tall man dropped something and they ran.

Page 12: Synthesis and Summary

1.

Mary Jane	Sarah
Parents did not see the point of school	Mother thought education important
Loved going to school	Did not like going to school
40 in a class	24 in class
(Everyone) worked hard	Did not do much work
Teacher very strict	Teacher never told anyone off
Sat in rows	Sat in groups
Not allowed to talk	Talked all the time
Liked the teacher	Did not like the teacher
Respected the teacher	Did not respect the teacher
Appreciated/valued school	Did not appreciate/value school

[1] for each pair up to a maximum of **[10]**

2. Look at the mark scheme below, decide which description is closest to your answer and then decide what mark to give it up to a maximum of **[4]**.

Marks	Skills
4	• You have shown clear understanding of both texts. • You have synthesised evidence from texts. • You have used a range of relevant detail from both texts.
3	• You have shown some understanding of both texts. • You have shown clear connections between texts. • You have used relevant detail from both texts.

Page 13: Referring to the Text

1. a–e, b–d, c–f   **[maximum 3]**
2. a) Macbeth refers to the prophecies as 'happy prologues'. **[2]**
   b) He tells us that one of them has come true: 'I am Thane of Cawdor.' **[2]**
   c) Macbeth asks how the prophecies can be evil when the witches have told the truth:

   > If ill,
   > Why hath it given me earnest of success
   > Commencing in a truth? **[2]**

3.

Point	Frankenstein's response is negative from the start.
Evidence	Referring to the experiment as a 'catastrophe' and his creation as a 'wretch'
Explanation	suggests that he has rejected the creature and will not try to find any good in it.

[maximum 3]

Page 14: Analysing Language 1

1. a) dialectical (also colloquial)   b) formal
   c) colloquial   d) technical   **[maximum 4]**

2. a) adjective   b) preposition
   c) conjunction   d) (concrete) noun
   e) adverb   f) verb   **[maximum 6]**

3. a) complex   b) Jo, Beth or Amy
   c) passive   d) past perfect
   e) third person   **[maximum 5]**

Page 15: Analysing Language 2

1. a) Simile. It suggests he ran extremely quickly as the wind travels quickly. **[2]** b) Metaphor. It suggests that there are a lot of insects and that they are dangerous, violent and organised. **[2]** c) Both. 'Heart' is a metaphor for her feelings/emotions. Describing it as cold or frozen suggests that she feels nothing.   **[maximum 6]**

2. a) Time b) fizzed/crackled   **[maximum 2]**
3. Look at the mark scheme below, decide which description is closest to your answer and then decide what mark to give it up to a maximum of **[5]**.

Marks	Skills
5	• You have made accurate and perceptive comments about the text. • You have analysed the effects of the choice of language. • You have used well-considered subject terminology accurately.
4	• You have given accurate impressions. • You have begun to analyse the choice of language. • You have used relevant subject terminology appropriately.

Page 16: Analysing Form and Structure

1. Up to **[2]** for any reasonable answer to each question up to a maximum of **[10]**.
   a) A boarding house / in a city / a place where single people rent rooms / Second Avenue (New York / America).
   b) 'Small and unobtrusive' / dressed plainly / shy / does not draw attention to herself / not interested in what's going on.
   c) Does not fit with the previous description of her / a change in mood / shows an interest in Andy / shows that she is sharp or intelligent / suggests she is judging him.
   d) He is polite or well-mannered / he has charm / he is starting a successful career / he is shallow or superficial / he is not interested in Miss Conway.
   e) She does something to make herself noticed / they get to know each other / they fall in love / they argue / it turns out that they know each other / any other reasonable conjecture.

2. a–y, b–z, c–x
                       [1] for each up to a maximum of **[3]**

English Language 1 – pages 17–20
Page 17: Reading Literature 1

1.

A naive/unreliable narrator	A
An omniscient narrator	D
A reliable first-person narrator	B
An intrusive narrator	C (also omniscient)

[2] for each up to a maximum of **[8]**

Page 18: Reading Literature 2

[1] for each correct answer in 'How we learn' and up to **[2]** for a reasonable explanation in 'What we learn' up to a maximum of **[15]**.

1.

Character	How we learn	What we learn
Hyde's housekeeper:	a)	She is a bad person / she cannot be trusted / she is polite.
Magwitch:	b)	He is aggressive / rough / frightening.
Darcy:	e)	People are generally impressed by him when they first meet him but quickly change their minds because of the way he behaves.
Mrs Reed:	d)	She is bad-tempered / aggressive / cruel / uncaring.
Victor Frankenstein:	c)	He is behaving strangely / he is sick / he is hysterical. He worries his friend.

Page 19: Creative Writing 1

The following answers are examples of the sort of thing you might write. Your own answers might be completely different. **[1]** for each reasonable answer.

1. **a)** First person; yes. **b)** Formal, using Standard English. **c)** Female **d)** 82 **e)** Small, neat, well-dressed **f)** Grew up on a farm and married a farmer, now living in a bungalow in a village **g)** A widow, with two children who live abroad, friendly with the neighbours but no close friends **h)** Speaks in a Cornish accent but uses Standard English **i)** walking and bird watching **j)** keeps her opinions to herself but hates being told what to do. **[maximum 10]**
2. **a)** In the village post office. **b)** Yes, she goes abroad. **c)** Now. **d)** A year. **e)** Yes (except for some memories in flashback). **[maximum 5]**
3. **Exposition**: Doris leads a quiet life in a small village with her two cats. **Inciting incident**: She wins the lottery. She decides to visit her children but not tell them she's a millionaire. **Turning point**: She goes to see her daughter in France, who is too busy to be bothered. She books her a ticket to Australia. In Australia her son lets her stay but after a while he puts her in a horrible home. **Climax**: She buys the nursing home, improves the lives of its patients and returns home, where she spends the rest of her money on herself and on charities. **Coda/ending**: Doris is living happily in the village with her cats and a man she met in the nursing home. She has spent all her money and not given any to her children. **[maximum 5]**

Page 20: Creative Writing 2

The following answers are examples of the sort of thing you might write. Your own answers will be completely different. **[1]** for each reasonable answer up to a maximum of **[20]** overall.

1. **a)** Arnold Spence
   b) A fairground in Australia.
2. **Character – a)** grey hair/woollen cardigan **b)** Scottish accent/cough **c)** aftershave/cough sweets **d)** not applicable **e)** rough hands/soft wool.
   Scene – a) Gaudy rides, milling crowds. **b)** Screeching child, loud dance music. **c)** Spicy sausage, burning wood. **d)** Tangy mustard, sweet toffee. **e)** Sticky candyfloss, slimy mud.
3. **Character – a)** a group of elderly people gathered around the television **b)** straight-backed smartly dressed gentleman **c)** startlingly white dentures.
   Scene – a) A blur of swirling colours and harsh noises. **b)** Candy-striped stall; fluffy toys piled high. **c)** Blue nylon fur, plastic brown eyes.
4. **Character – a)** like a leopard amongst domestic cats **b)** a whirlwind of activity.
   Scene – a) The crowd rumbled and rolled like a storm-tossed ship. **b)** An explosion of excited laughter.

English Language 2 – pages 21–22

Page 21: Reading Non-fiction

1. Up to **[2]** for each answer similar to the following up to a maximum of **[20]**:

	Text A	Text B
What is the writer's attitude to Little Mickledon?	Likes it. Finds it 'charming and tranquil'.	Does not like the peace and quiet: 'totally cut off'.
What is the writer's opinion of the B & B?	Finds it 'delightful' and gives positive impression of the owners.	Finds it a 'disappointment', criticises several aspects and does not like owners' attitude.
What impression do you get of the writer?	Someone who likes peace and quiet. Someone who focuses on positive aspects.	Someone who likes to be in touch. Someone who likes to criticise / likes to find fault.

How would you describe the general tone and style?	Positive/enthusiastic/vague	Negative/critical/honest
Comment on language features.	Uses words like 'relax', 'calm' and 'tranquil' to give an impression of peace and quiet. Uses archaic words/spellings (Olde, yore) and puts quotation marks round 'civilization'.	Colloquial – addresses readers with imperative ('Be warned'). Uses adjectives to give an unflattering picture: 'grubby', 'pitiful', 'hippy'.

Page 22: Persuasive/Transactional Writing

1. The following are only suggestions. There are many other points you could make. **[1]** for each up to a maximum of **[10]**.

Pros	Cons
Studying for exams is much more important.	It helps you understand the importance of things like punctuality and politeness.
The work being done is not interesting or meaningful.	It helps you choose your future career.
Students on work experience are just free labour.	You can learn new skills.
In the time you cannot get a realistic idea of what the work is like.	You might make contacts which would lead to paid employment.
You've got the rest of your life to experience work.	You get to meet a wide range of people.

2. **[1]** for each of the following up to a maximum of **[5]**:
   - opening with 'Dear Sir' or 'Dear Editor'
   - setting out the opening correctly
   - using a formal tone
   - clearly stating the purpose of your letter
   - putting your point of view strongly and clearly
   - using a rhetorical or literary device
   - accurate spelling and punctuation.

3. **[1]** for each of the following up to a maximum of **[5]**:
   - using an intriguing/amusing headline
   - using a strapline
   - using an appropriate informal tone
   - clearly stating the purpose of your article
   - putting your point of view strongly and clearly
   - using a rhetorical or literary device
   - accurate spelling and punctuation.

Shakespeare – pages 23–24

Page 23: Context and Themes

1. Up to **[2]** for each reasonable answer up to a maximum of **[12]**.
2. Up to **[2]** for each reasonable answer up to a maximum of **[12]**.

Page 24: Characters, Language and Structure

1. **[2]** for each quotation and **[2]** for a reasonable interpretation up to a maximum of **[12]**.
2. **[1]** for each correct answer and up to **[2]** for a reasonable explanation similar to the suggestions below up to a maximum of **[12]**.
   a) Oxymoron. Its use suggests confusion about love and how the themes of love and hate are intertwined in the play. **b)** Metaphor. The speaker (Shylock) picks up on an insulting comparison and extends it to warn that he can 'bite.' **c)** Rhetorical question. The chorus asks whether it is

(Continued)

possible to recreate the war in a theatre. He is challenging the audience and hoping to prove that the answer is 'yes'.
c) Pathetic fallacy / personification.
Othello makes the rocks and hills seem alive, making his description more vivid and impressive.

Poetry – pages 25–28

Page 25: Context and Themes
1. **a)** 'Death of a Naturalist' [1] **b)** 'Living Space' [1]
   c) Sonnet 43 [1] **d)** Excerpt from 'The Prelude' [1] **e)** 'Mametz Wood' [1]
2. The following answers are suggestions. You may have listed other poems. [1] for each title listed appropriately, up to a maximum of [16].
   a) 'The Prelude'; 'Hawk Roosting'; Death of a Naturalist'.
   b) 'To Autumn'; 'The Prelude'; 'As Imperceptibly as Grief'; 'She Walks in Beauty'.
   c) 'Living Space'; 'London'; 'A Wife in London'.
   d) Sonnet 43; 'Cozy Apologia'; 'The Manhunt'; 'She Walks in Beauty'.
   e) 'Dulce et Decorum Est'; 'The Soldier'; 'The Manhunt; 'London'; 'Mametz Wood'.
   f) 'The Manhunt'; 'A Wife in London'.
   g) 'Death of a Naturalist'; 'The Prelude'; 'Afternoons'.
   h) 'Afternoons'; 'Death of a Naturalist'; 'The Prelude'; Sonnet 43.

Page 26: Language, Form and Structure
1. [1] for each technique identified and [1] for each reasonable explanation (the explanations below are suggestions only), up to a maximum of [36].
   a) Caesura, archaic language. The use of 'thee' makes it sound almost religious. The caesura makes the reader stop as the poet stops to think. [4]
   b) Onomatopoeia, simile, caesura, enjambment. Onomatopoeia gives a 'sound picture' of the comic brutality of the frogs. The simile associates them with war, making them the enemy. The combination of caesura and enjambment means the poem is broken up in an irregular, disturbing way. [8]
   c) Personification. This makes the season sound like a young girl who only stays briefly. [2]
   d) Alliteration, metaphor. Manacles are used to restrain prisoners. Blake's metaphor says that they are made in the mind. Whether the minds of those who are

oppressed or those who are oppressing is not clear. The alliteration emphasises his point and gives an almost numbing sound. [4]
   e) Alliteration (sibilance), simile, rhyming couplet, end-stopping. The sibilance reflects the gentle feelings described, contrasting with the traditional simile of 'arrows' to denote the pain of love. The rhyming couplets reflect the simplicity of the feeling and the end-stopping shows confidence in the feeling expressed. [8]
   f) Repetition/enjambment. The sentence runs across two stanzas, showing how things continue. This is emphasised by the repetition of the phrase 'courting-places'. The wind is seen almost as a person, deliberately spoiling things. [6]
   g) Alliteration, simile/personification. The woman is associated with the beauty of nature and the mystery of the night. The alliteration conveys a calm, gentle feeling. This feeling is reinforced by the use of enjambment. [6]

Page 27: Unseen Poetry
1. Up to [2] for each answer similar to those below. Other answers might be equally valid.
   a) It is set in a forest during a storm.
   b) No, it is irregular (free verse). The lack of regular patterns reflects the unpredictability of the storm.
   c) 'Cackle with uncouth sounds' conveys the harshness of the sounds described. It could be called onomatopoeia.
   d) In 'white liquid fire, bright white' the 'i's are sharp and quick, like the lightning.
   e) Describing the lightning as a 'white snake' adds a sense of danger as well as painting a vivid picture.
   f) By adding a lot of details in this simple way, the poet builds a sense of the way the storm continues and shows no sign of stopping.
   g) The repetition of this phrase and the shortness of the line give it greater impact, emphasising that humans may think they have harnessed the power of electricity but they cannot really tame nature.
   h) The power and wonder of nature – the insignificance of humans – the arrogance of humans.
   i) He is in awe of nature – he is excited and perhaps frightened by the storm – it makes him feel insignificant – it makes him realise that humans are not really powerful.
   j) Any answer rooted in the text. [maximum 20]

Page 28: Unseen Poetry
2. The answers below are suggestions. There may be other valid responses. Up to [2] for every box filled in with a reasonable response, up to a maximum of [32].

	'Storm in the Black Forest'	'The Vixen'
Setting (time and place)	In a forest during a storm.	In the woods on what seems to be a typical day for the vixen.
What happens in the poem	The poet describes the stages of a violent storm and how it never seems to end, making him think about man and nature.	The poet describes the behaviour of a vixen and her cubs, and how she reacts to danger.
Structure	Four stanzas of unequal lengths (one of only one line) and lines of different lengths, giving a sense of unpredictability.	One stanza of 14 lines, describing what happens in a controlled way. 14 lines, as in a sonnet, but not sonnet structure.
Rhythm and rhyme	No regularity – again reflecting the storm.	Iambic pentameter – smooth and regular. Rhyming couplets – simple structure, each couplet describing one small action.
Vocabulary/register	Language of richness (bronzey), danger (snake), movement (wriggling) and science (electric) combine to convey awe and wonder.	Everyday, straightforward language.

Use of sound	Alliteration and assonance used to suggest the sounds of the storm.	Sounds made by vixen conveyed by onomatopoeia. Alliteration in line 13.
Imagery	Metaphor and personification used to give vivid impression of the power of the storm.	Literal imagery: the poem describes the scene.
Themes and the poet's attitude	The power of nature; the arrogance of man; the wonder of nature. The last stanza draws a 'lesson' from the experience. He is excited and frightened by nature and impressed by its power. He feels humans are comparatively powerless, though they think they are powerful.	Tension between nature and man; motherhood; the beauty of nature. He is impressed by the vixen's care for her cubs. He sees the danger posed by humans from her point of view. The ending gives a positive, hopeful view of life.

Post-1914 Prose/Drama – pages 29–30

Page 29: Context and Themes

Below are examples of the kind of answer you might have given. Up to **[5]** for each reasonable answer similar to these, depending on how full your answer is.

1. a) *An Inspector Calls* is set shortly before the First World War, in 1912, in a 'large city' in the Midlands. The family is middle-class and wealthy, Mr Birling being a self-made man who has married someone from a higher social class. They are 'comfortable' and smug but the Inspector reveals the dark underside of their world.

    b) The world of *Never Let Me Go* seems to be just like the real world of just a few years ago. However, there are aspects of this world which are not real (as far as we know). Breeding people to provide spare parts is not something that is done officially now, although there are cases of people having children to provide genetic material for existing children who are sick.

    c) *Blood Brothers* was originally written to be performed for schools and youth groups on Merseyside. This is reflected in the simple plot, the characters and the issues. It later became a musical. The use of songs to express feelings or advance the plot reflects the tradition of musical theatre.

2. a) **[1]** for each theme up to a maximum of **[4]**.
    b) Up to **[2]** for each reasonable answer up to a maximum of **[8]**.

Page 30: Characters, Language and Structure

1. **[1]** for every box completed with a reasonable answer up to a maximum of **[24]**.

2. Up to **[2]** for each reasonable answer up to a maximum of **[10]**.

Nineteenth-Century Prose – pages 31–32

Page 31: Context and Themes

1. Up to **[2]** for each reasonable answer up to a maximum of **[10]**.

2. a) **[1]** for each reasonable answer up to a maximum of **[5]**.
    b) Up to **[2]** for each reasonable answer up to a maximum of **[10]**.

Page 32: Characters, Language and Structure

1. **[1]** for every box completed with a reasonable answer up to a maximum of **[25]**.
2. a–x, b–v, c–y, d–z, e–w **[2]** for each correct answer up to a maximum of **[10]**

Practice Exam Papers – pages 33–64

Page 34 English Language Component 1

Section A: Reading

A1 • mirrors
    • cakes
    • sweetmeats
    • chocolates
    • wedding cake.
    [1] for each up to a maximum of **[5]**

A2 Look at the mark scheme below, decide which description is closest to your answer and then decide what mark to give it up to a maximum of **[5]**.

Marks	Skills
5	• You have made accurate and perceptive comments about what makes the shop window attractive. • You have analysed the effects of the choice of language. • You have used well-considered subject terminology accurately.
4	• You have made accurate comments about what makes the shop window attractive. • You have begun to analyse the choice of language. • You have used relevant subject terminology appropriately.

You might have included some of the following points in your answer:

*   The word 'rainbow' is used to show how colourful it is; it has connotations of happiness (sun after rain).
*   It is 'natural' for the window to attract children – maybe adults as well.
*   There may be an implication that he is child-like in his wonder.
*   'Fiery charm' suggests warmth and passion.
*   The attraction is not just the sweets, hinting that there is something or someone else attracting him to the shop.
*   Litotes (ironic understatement) is used to tell us that the chocolates are still part of the attraction: he 'was far from despising' them.

A3 Look at the mark scheme below, decide which description is closest to your answer and then decide which mark to give yourself up to a maximum of **[10]**

Marks	Skills
9–10	• You have made accurate and perceptive comments about the text. • You have given a detailed analysis of how the writer uses language to achieve effects. • You have chosen an appropriate range of examples. • You have used well-considered subject terminology accurately to support your comments.
7–8	• You have made accurate comments about the text. • You have begun to analyse how the writer uses language to achieve effects. • You have chosen appropriate examples. • You have used relevant subject terminology accurately to support your comments.

In your answer you might have made some of the following points:

- The writer gives his background, establishing something about his character and what he does.
- There is a physical description – 'Tall, burly, red-haired', three adjectives giving a clear picture.
- There is a contradiction between his 'resolute face' and his 'listless manner'.
- His face makes him seem determined, but he behaves in a relaxed way.
- He is an artist – he has sketches with him – and makes some money (but not a lot) from them.
- He comes from a rich family but will not inherit their money.
- He is involved in politics (Socialism).
- He is polite to the young lady in the shop.
- The statement that he 'merely' raises his hat suggests that he might be expected to be friendlier towards her.

A4 Look at the mark scheme below, decide which description is closest to your answer and then decide which mark to give yourself up to a maximum of [10].

Marks	Skills
9–10	• You have made accurate and perceptive comments about the text. • You have given a detailed analysis of how the writer uses language and the organisation of events (structure) to achieve effects. • You have chosen an appropriate range of examples. • You have used well-considered subject terminology accurately to support your comments.
7–8	• You have made accurate comments about how details are used. • You have begun to analyse how the writer uses language and the organisation of events (structure) to achieve effects. • You have chosen appropriate examples. • You have used relevant subject terminology accurately to support your comments.

In your answer you might have made some of the following points:

- Their first encounter is casual yet polite, as we might expect from a customer and a waitress.
- The short sentence 'His order was evidently a usual one' establishes him as a 'regular' and the visit to the shop as part of his routine.
- At this stage the woman has not been given a name. We do not know how well he knows her.
- His casual proposal comes as a surprise – it could be a joke or it could be serious.
- She takes control by saying she doesn't 'allow' such remarks.
- She seems to see the proposal as a joke – the reader would probably agree.
- The man suddenly looks serious, changing the tone and suggesting it is not a joke.
- However, his comparison of love to a bun is comical.
- Her reaction is intriguing. She is 'studying' and seems 'tragic', giving a serious turn to the story.
- The 'shadow of a smile' suggests she is interested, as does sitting down. It is now clear this is not just a customer/waitress relationship.
- Angus remains frivolous but returns to the subject of marriage.
- There is contrast between what they say and the looks they give each other.

A5 Look at the mark scheme below, decide which description is closest to your answer and then decide which mark to give yourself up to a maximum of [10].

Marks	Skills
9–10	• You have persuasively evaluated the text and its effects. • You have used convincing, well-selected examples from the text to explain your views. • Your response shows engagement and involvement, taking an overview and making comments on the text as a whole. • You have explored with insight how the writer has created thoughts and feelings.
7–8	• You have critically evaluated the text and its effects. • You have used well-selected examples from the text to explain your views. • Your response shows critical awareness and clear engagement with the text. • You have explored how the writer has created thoughts and feelings.

In your answer you may have mentioned some of the following points:

- We are not told what she is thinking about except that she is 'not unsympathetic' – so perhaps she returns his feelings.
- The revelation of what she thinks or feels is delayed by his actions.
- She continues to try to do her job – there is tension between this and her relationship with Angus.
- He calls her 'dear Laura', showing that there is some kind of friendship/relationship between them.
- However, she tells him not to talk 'like that': it is not clear whether she thinks he is being over-friendly.
- She is exasperated with him and his manner, but she tries to stay in control of the situation. She has, so far, been the object of the young man's attention but towards the end of the passage the focus is much more on her.
- There is a feeling we might now learn what she has been thinking about and how she feels about Angus.

Page 37 English Language Component 1

Section B: Writing

Look at the mark scheme below, decide which description is closest to your answer and then decide which mark to give yourself. This task is marked for communication and organisation, and for technical accuracy.

Communication and Organisation (maximum 24)

Marks	Skills
20–24	• Your writing is fully coherent and controlled. Plot and characterisation are developed with detail, originality and imagination. • Your writing is clearly and imaginatively organised. The narrative is sophisticated and fully engages the reader's interest. • You have used structure and grammatical features ambitiously to give the writing cohesion and coherence. • You have communicated ambitiously and consistently to convey precise meaning.
15–19	• Your writing is clear and controlled. Plot and characterisation show convincing detail, and some originality and imagination. • Your writing is clearly organised. The narrative is purposefully shaped and developed. • You have used structure and grammatical features to give the writing cohesion and coherence. • You have communicated with some ambition to convey precise meaning.

Vocabulary, sentence structure, spelling and punctuation (maximum 16)

Marks	Skills
14–16	• You have used appropriate and effective variations in sentence structure. • Virtually all your sentence construction is controlled and accurate. • You have used a range of punctuation confidently and accurately. • You have spelled almost all words, including complex and irregular words, correctly. • Your control of tense and agreement is totally secure. • You have used a wide range of appropriate, ambitious vocabulary to create precise meaning.
11–13	• You have used varied sentence structure. • Your sentence construction is secure. • You have used a range of punctuation accurately. • You have spelled most words, including irregular words, correctly. • Your control of tense and agreement is secure. • You have used a range of ambitious vocabulary with precision.

Page 41 English Language Component 2

Section A: Reading

A1 a) children [1] b) under 300 [1] c) six [1]

A2 Look at the mark scheme below, decide which description is closest to your answer and then decide what mark to give it up to a maximum of [10].

Marks	Skills
9–10	• You have given a persuasive evaluation of the text and its effects. • You have supported your evaluation with convincing, well-selected textual references. • You have shown engagement and involvement, taking an overview of the text to make perceptive comments.
7–8	• You have given a critical evaluation of the text and its effects. • You have supported your evaluation with well selected textual references. • You have shown clear awareness and critical engagement with the text.

You should have included some of the following points in your answer:
- The campaign has support from well-known people, including a writer.
- Frobisher says going to the library made her a writer.
- She and Gomez use persuasive arguments about the value of the library to the community.
- This aspect of the library's role is mentioned several times.
- The campaigners also refer to the importance of reading.
- The opposing argument is put for balance.
- The statistics about library use are quite convincing.
- More space is given to campaigners than opponents – and their actual words are reported.
- The impression is given that the campaign has a lot of support and the campaigners are very passionate and committed.

A3 (a) Support their campaign for public libraries [1] by voting for them [1]. (b) Most people understand why libraries are a good idea. [1]

A4 Look at the mark scheme below, decide which description is closest to your answer and then decide which mark to give it up to a maximum of [10].

Marks	Skills
9–10	• You have made accurate and perceptive comments about a wide range of different examples from the text. • You have given a detailed analysis of how the writer uses language and structure to achieve effects and influence readers. • You have used subject terminology accurately to support your comments.
7–8	• You have made accurate comments about a range of different examples from the text. • You have begun to analyse how the writer uses language and structure to influence readers. • You have used subject terminology to support your comments.

You should have included some of the following points in your answer:
- The tone is extremely polite and to a modern reader might even seem sycophantic, the writers signing off with 'We beg, Sir, to remain yours obediently'.
- They start with a question, which explains what they want in a very polite way.
- In the second paragraph they say what they are not going to do, giving the idea that people already agree with them.
- They give a long explanation, in the past tense, of the history of their libraries.
- They use statistics as evidence to impress the reader of their 'success', a word they keep repeating.
- The whole letter has a polite tone (for example, the use of modal verbs: 'May we be allowed'; 'We would').
- The use of long, complex sentences also makes the tone seem reasonable and polite.

A5 Look at the mark scheme below, decide which description is closest to your answer and then decide what mark to give it up to a maximum of [4].

Marks	Skills
4	• You have shown clear understanding of both texts. • You have synthesised evidence from texts. • You have used a range of relevant detail from both texts.
3	• You have shown some understanding of both texts. • You have shown clear connections between texts. • You have used relevant detail from both texts.

You might have included some or all of the following points:
- In 1891 the libraries in Marylebone are new, although the buildings they are in are unsuitable, one being 'plain and insufficient'.
- The King's Cross library, which was built over 100 years ago, is 'roomy' and 'generously proportioned'.
- The number of people using this library is falling, reflecting the fact that the area is not 'thriving'.
- In Marylebone in 1891, where the libraries are 'in two of the most populous parts of the parish', 'the demand increases daily'.
- The libraries in Marylebone are not funded by the council. King's Park is run by the council but the council does not want it.
- They also say it is only really pensioners who use it, whereas the Marylebone libraries are used by 'persons of all sorts and conditions'.

A6 Look at the mark scheme below, decide which description is closest to your answer and then decide which mark to give it up to a maximum of **[10]**.

Marks	Skills
9–10	• You have made comparisons that are sustained and detailed. • You have shown clear understanding of the methods used to convey ideas.
7–8	• You have made detailed comparisons. • You have made valid comments on how the ideas are conveyed.

You should have included some of the following points in your answer:
- The two texts have different purposes. The article's is to report on the campaign to save the library and the letter's is to persuade people to support public libraries.
- The article includes both direct and reported speech from several people who are trying to keep the library open and who use emotive language, such as 'heart' and 'devastating', together with personal anecdotes, clichés ('drop in the ocean') and rhetorical techniques such as rhetorical questions ('how can the Mayor…?') to persuade.
- The letter also uses rhetorical techniques but is more subtle. The letter starts by saying what it is NOT going to do, implying confidence that the argument for public libraries has been won.
- The letter's tone is calm and measured, its arguments backed by evidence. This is similar to the way the council spokesperson in the newspaper article puts her case.
- Witherspoon is reporting the views of others while Debenham and Hollond give their own point of view.

Page 42 English Language Component 2

Section B: Writing

B1 and B2 Look at the mark scheme below, decide which description is closest to your answer and then decide which mark to give yourself. This task is marked for communication and organisation, and for technical accuracy.

Communication and Organisation (maximum 12)

Marks	Skills
11–12	• Your writing shows sophisticated understanding of the purpose and format of the task. • Your writing shows sustained awareness of the reader/intended audience. • You have used an appropriate register, confidently adapted to purpose/audience. • Your content is ambitious, pertinent and sophisticated. • Your ideas are convincingly developed and supported by a range of relevant details.
8–10	• Your writing shows consistent understanding of the purpose and format of the task. • Your writing shows secure awareness of the reader/intended audience. • You have used an appropriate register, consistently adapted to purpose/audience. • Your content is well-judged and detailed. • Your ideas are organised and coherently developed, supported by relevant details.

Vocabulary, sentence structure, spelling and punctuation (maximum 8)

Marks	Skills
8	• You have used appropriate and effective variations in sentence structure. • Virtually all your sentence construction is controlled and accurate. • You have used a range of punctuation confidently and accurately. • You have spelled almost all words, including complex and irregular words, correctly. • Your control of tense and agreement is totally secure. • You have used a wide range of appropriate, ambitious vocabulary to create precise meaning.
6–7	• You have used varied sentence structure. • Your sentence construction is secure. • You have used a range of punctuation accurately. • You have spelled most words, including irregular words, correctly. • Your control of tense and agreement is secure. • You have used a range of vocabulary with precision.

Page 44 English Literature Component 1

Section A: Shakespeare

For all questions, look at the mark scheme below, decide which description is closest to your answer and then decide which mark to give yourself up to a maximum of **[15]** for part **a)** and **[20]** for part **b)**.

Marks	Skills
a) 13–15 b) 17–20	• You have sustained focus on the task, including an overview, and conveyed your ideas consistently and coherently. • You have approached the text sensitively and analysed it critically. • You have shown a perceptive understanding of the text, engaging with a personal response and some originality. • You have included pertinent quotations from the text. • You have analysed and appreciated the writer's use of language, form and structure. • You have used precise subject terminology appropriately.
a) 10–12 b) 13–16	• You have sustained focus on the task, including an overview, and conveyed your ideas coherently. • You have approached the text thoughtfully. • You have shown a secure understanding of key aspects of the text, with considerable engagement. • You have included well-chosen quotations from the text. • You have discussed and increasingly analysed the writer's use of language, form and structure. • You have used subject terminology appropriately.

Part **(b)** is also marked for spelling, punctuation, vocabulary and sentence structure [maximum 5].

Marks	Skills
4–5	• You have spelled and punctuated with consistent accuracy. • You have consistently used vocabulary and sentence structure to achieve effective control of meaning.
2–3	• You have spelled and punctuated with considerable accuracy. • You have consistently used a considerable vocabulary and sentence structure to achieve general control of meaning.

Your answers could include some of the following points.

1. *Macbeth*

   (a)
   • Macbeth is seen here preparing for battle; he is a soldier again.
   • Speaking in soliloquy, he says he has no fear.
   • He is aware of what he has done.
   • Ambiguity in 'she should have died hereafter'.
   • Repetition of 'tomorrow' and imagery used to describe time.
   • Imagery conveys one man's insignificance and the pointlessness of life.

   (b)
   • Lady Macbeth may be more ruthless than Macbeth, blaming the guards for Duncan's murder.
   • She persuades him to murder Duncan.
   • She embraces evil; he knows he is doing wrong.
   • He discusses his guilt; hers seems not to affect her until the sleepwalking scene.
   • As a woman she only has power through him, but she dominates him and taunts him about his role as a man.

2. *Romeo and Juliet*

   (a)
   • Juliet's desire for Romeo to stay, pretending it is still night.
   • Imagery of light and dark – they can only be together in the dark.
   • The marriage is consummated and so is a real marriage – important later in the play.
   • Romeo's use of nature imagery/personification.
   • Imagery reflects the enormity of their passion.
   • Awareness of danger – love and death.

   (b)
   • Contrast with his love for Rosaline.
   • His soliloquies expressing his feelings.
   • The sonnet used to express mutual love
   • The imagery he uses to express his feelings.
   • Portrayal of his love and their relationship in the balcony scene.
   • His commitment to her and his actions after their marriage.
   • Association of love and death.
   • Marriage as holy – spiritual and sexual fulfilment.
   • Nurse's disregard for the sanctity of marriage as well as for Juliet's feelings.

3. *Henry V*

   (a)
   • Contrast of comic scene/characters with previous scene.
   • Characters once associated with Falstaff and Henry in his youth, but now rejected by Henry.
   • Boy's rejection of them echoes this.
   • They are inspired by Henry's speech, repeating 'the breach' and are determined to fight.
   • They sing and fight, behaving as if they are in a tavern, not on a battlefield.
   • Fluellen is wild and violent – a stereotypical Welshman of the time.

   (b)
   • He can be ruthless as well as statesmanlike.
   • He can also be clever and diplomatic.
   • He inspires his men before Agincourt.
   • He is seen as a war leader and a successful king.
   • A more human/ordinary side is seen in his interactions with soldiers and his wooing of Katherine.

4. *The Merchant of Venice*

   (a)
   • He sees Antonio as a 'fool' for lending without interest, recalling that moneylenders had to be outsiders.
   • He has no interest in appearing merciful as society might expect.
   • Repetition of 'my bond' shows anger.
   • He recalls his former treatment by Antonio.
   • Calling him a dog implies Jews are seen as less than human.
   • The jailer has allowed Antonio to 'come abroad' – Antonio, the insider, is not seen as a criminal.

   (b)
   • The Doge's role in the trial. Can it be fair?
   • Shylock's demands for justice and his 'bond'.
   • Portia's speech about mercy.
   • The failure of Portia's appeal to Shylock and what this says about him.
   • Is the outcome of the trial just?
   • How far would differences in Elizabethan and modern attitudes influence an audience's reaction to the trial?

5. *Much Ado About Nothing*

   (a)
   • Benedick has not yet appeared, but we anticipate a clash and/or romance with Beatrice.
   • Beatrice asks if he is with Don Pedro, indicating an interest in him.
   • Something happened the last time they met but we never know exactly what.
   • Contrast between the messenger's account of Benedick as a 'good soldier' and Beatrice's.
   • She does not seem to want to hear anything good about him.
   • Leonato's reference to a 'merry war' makes us expect battles of wits – but is there real dislike or is it all a joke?

   (b)
   • Different definitions of 'honour': chastity; reputation; family responsibilities.
   • Claudio does not behave honourably to Hero though he rejects her because he thinks she has lost her honour.
   • Benedick is not obliged to defend Hero but doing so shows his love for Beatrice.
   • It also shows that he understands 'honour' as being a matter of right and wrong, not loyalty to friends.
   • Honour is associated with the court and the aristocracy. Claudio has not behaved as a man of his class is expected to.

6. *Othello*

   (a)
   • The audience may still be shocked by the killing of Desdemona.
   • After attacking Iago, Othello is calm.
   • He does not want to make excuses: 'nothing extenuate'.
   • He blames his passion and his love.
   • He still has pride in his achievements.
   • Audience members may feel a range of emotions.

   (b)
   • Iago is the opposite of Othello, but Othello is still quick to believe his wife is unfaithful.
   • Because of his soliloquies the audience is drawn into Iago's plans.
   • As they progress we see the effects of his dishonesty and ruthlessness.

- He is reminiscent of the 'devils' of medieval plays, who spoke to the audience about their villainy.
- His motives are not always clear – Jealousy? Revenge? Racism?
- His relationship with Emilia can be compared to Othello and Desdemona's marriage.

Page 50 English Literature Component 1

Section B: Poetry

1. For both parts of the question, look at the mark scheme below, decide which description is closest to your answer and then decide which mark to give yourself. Mark part **(a)** out of **15** and part **(b)** out of **25**.

Marks	Skills
(a) 13–15 **(b)** 21–25	• You have sustained focus on the task, including an overview, and conveyed your ideas consistently and coherently. • You have approached the text sensitively and analysed it critically. • You have shown a perceptive understanding of the text, engaging with a personal response and some originality. • You have included pertinent quotations from the text. • You have analysed and appreciated the writer's use of language, form and structure. • You have used precise subject terminology appropriately. • You have shown an assured understanding of the relationships between texts and the contexts in which they were written. • (part b) only) You have made critical and illuminating comparisons throughout. • (part b) only) There is a wide ranging discussion of the similarities and differences.
(a) 10–12 **(b)** 16–20	• You have sustained focus on the task, including an overview, and conveyed your ideas coherently. • You have approached the text thoughtfully. • You have shown a secure understanding of key aspects of the text, with considerable engagement. • You have included well-chosen quotations from the text. • You have discussed and increasingly analysed the writer's use of language, form and structure. • You have used subject terminology appropriately. • You have shown a secure understanding of the relationships between texts and the contexts in which they were written. • (part b) only) You have made focussed and coherent comparisons throughout. • (part b) only) There is a clear discussion of the similarities and differences.

Your answer might include:

(a)
- The poet witnesses the suffering but is not personally involved.
- Suffering is both physical and psychological.
- Regularity of form, metre and rhyme.
- Ballad form – return to simple forms in Romantic movement.
- Effect of use of repetition.
- Suffering caused by the powerful – others are victims.
- Urban setting, in the context of the industrial revolution and the growth of cities.
- Angry tone.
- The politics of the French Revolution and their influence on Romanticism shown here.

(b)
- Possible comparison with 'Living Space', focussing on suffering in an urban environment and the powerlessness of ordinary people.
- Compare with 'Dulce et Decorum Est' or 'The Manhunt' where suffering is the result of war.
- Compare ideas of power with 'Hawk Roosting' or 'Ozymandias'.
- Compare the use of regular form with 'Ozymandias' or 'Hawk Roosting'
- Compare the use of an outsider observing suffering to 'A Wife in London'/ 'Mametz Wood'.
- Contrast with the personal involvement of the poet in 'Dulce et Decorum Est' or the persona in 'The Manhunt'.

Page 52 English Literature Component 2

Section A: Post-1914 Prose/Drama

22–31. Look at the mark scheme below, decide which description is closest to your answer and then decide which mark to give yourself.

Marks	Skills
29–35	• You have sustained focus on the task, including an overview, and conveyed your ideas consistently and coherently. • You have approached the text sensitively and analysed it critically. • You have shown a perceptive understanding of the text, engaging with a personal response and some originality. • You have included pertinent quotations from the text. • You have analysed and appreciated the writer's use of language, form and structure. • You have used precise subject terminology appropriately.
22–28	• You have sustained focus on the task, including an overview, and conveyed your ideas coherently. • You have approached the text thoughtfully. • You have shown a secure understanding of key aspects of the text, with considerable engagement. • You have included well-chosen quotations from the text. • You have discussed and increasingly analysed the writer's use of language, form and structure. • You have used subject terminology appropriately.

This question is also marked for accuracy in spelling, punctuation and the use of vocabulary and sentence structures. **[5 marks]**

Marks	Skills
4–5	• You have spelled and punctuated with consistent accuracy. • You have consistently used vocabulary and sentence structure to achieve effective control of meaning.
2–3	• You have spelled and punctuated with considerable accuracy. • You have consistently used a considerable vocabulary and sentence structure to achieve general control of meaning.

[Maximum 35 + 5 = 40 marks]

Your answers could include some of the following points.

1. *An Inspector Calls*
   - Eva Smith as a representative of the working class.
   - Is she one person or several people? In the extract the Inspector refers to 'several names'.

- He gives shocking details of her death, invoking horror and sympathy.
- The Inspector establishes her connection to the Birlings in the extract, but Arthur Birling is dismissive.
- To him she is just one of 'several hundred young women'.
- The Inspector shows the photo to the Birlings separately.
- She is involved with all the Birlings.
- The situations she is in are almost stereotypical.
- The Birlings' treatment of her reveals their characters and attitudes.

2. *Blood Brothers*
   - The fact of their being brothers demonstrates the importance of class in their futures.
   - They behave and speak differently. This is shown clearly in the extract.
   - Some of the tension in the extract comes from class differences, but some from the situation and Edward's mother's reactions.
   - Irony in 'you're not the same as him'.
   - Edward has opportunities that Mickey does not have.
   - Is it just money or is there more to class?
   - There does not seem to be any social mobility in the play.
   - The differences between them are quite crudely drawn.
   - The two boys are not different in nature – their differences are the result of upbringing.

3. *The History Boys*
   - In the extract Irwin is shown as television presenter/popular historian.
   - His language is deliberately shocking, as are the points he makes.
   - His focus on the toilets could be seen as making history more real or as appealing to the lowest common denominator.
   - It is history as entertainment.
   - Why has Bennett made the choice to have all the boys studying history (unlikely in real life)?
   - Is it just a way of passing exams?
   - Mrs Lintott and Irwin have different approaches. Irwin wants to question everything.
   - Is this any better than accepting everything?
   - The idea that there is 'no need to tell the truth'.
   - Irwin's subsequent career involves him in making history.

4. *The Curious Incident of the Dog in the Night-Time*
   - Christopher accepts his father's version of events, as does the audience at first.
   - His desire to solve the mystery leads him to the truth.
   - Judy speaks through letters.
   - Her version of events is very different.
   - In the extract she makes calm reasonable points about why Christopher is better off with his father.
   - She then tells a long anecdote, showing what it was like to take him out.
   - She is using this to justify her actions – would she gain the audience's sympathy here?
   - She gives the other side of living with Christopher, admitting she could not cope.
   - She presents a nostalgic view of family life.
   - In the end she returns and commits to Christopher.

5. *A Taste of Honey*
   - The mother–daughter relationship is central.
   - In the extract the writer establishes a relationship that is more like a friendship.
   - Jo is more like the adult, looking after Helen.
   - The story about Helen's ex-boyfriend shows that Jo has romantic crushes on men.
   - Reference to the flowers shows a creative side/a longing for something different.
   - She argues with her mother about everything and resents their way of life.
   - She knows nothing about her father and is worried by what her mother tells her about him.
   - There is a role-reversal, Jo seemingly more mature than Helen.

- Jo is critical of her mother but puts up with her.
- Jo is motivated by not wanting to be like her mother.
- She feels she can do without her but in the end has no-one else.

6. *Lord of the Flies*
   - Golding's characters are English public schoolboys, representatives of the 'civilised' world.
   - At first they behave as they would expect adults to, electing a leader and making rules.
   - Rivalries, fights, etc. are usual in schools but here they get out of hand.
   - The role of Jack and the hunters.
   - In the extract, words like 'tribe' and 'savages' are used to describe the hunters.
   - Jack is naked apart from paint and a belt.
   - They are starting to enjoy killing rather than just killing for food.
   - Jack and his 'tribe' have rejected the civilisation created on the island by Ralph and others.
   - The symbolism of the conch and the beast.
   - Changes in the way the boys speak.
   - Stages in the escalation of violence: killing the pig, Piggy, Simon.
   - What happens at the end? Has civilisation broken down or have we just learned how superficial the idea is?

7. *Never Let Me Go*
   - They are called guardians, not teachers. What is the difference?
   - In some ways they act like conventional teachers, but some things they do – such as the 'sex lectures' or the gallery – are odd.
   - They know about the children's future but only give little bits of information.
   - They are part of the system and controlled by the system.
   - Miss Geraldine is the most popular guardian and is a stereotype of the popular female teacher.
   - Miss Lucy's talks with Tommy show her doubts about the school. She is 'idealistic'.
   - In the extract Miss Lucy talks on the surface like a teacher speaking to a pupil but there is something mysterious and disturbing about what she says.
   - Here Tommy starts to realise the guardians may not be what they seem.
   - Her 'shaking' is disturbing. She is angry but not at Tommy – so what is she angry about?
   - Miss Emily's views are ambiguous. She works within society as it is.

8. *Anita and Me*
   - Some of the neighbours' behaviour is casual, even unknowing, racism.
   - The dog's name causes Meena to question racist language: 'it's like a swear word'.
   - Sam's behaviour at the fete is more openly racist – Meena feels personally hurt.
   - Meena's mother and her friends talk about English people in a way that could be thought racist.
   - In the extract, racist language is used against Meena's mother.
   - This is a shock to Meena but not to her mother.
   - She realises it is part of everyday life for her family and explains how it makes her feel.
   - Racist violence against Aunty Usha is reported and Sam's racism culminates in beating up Mr Bhatra.
   - The reference to 'Paki bashing' suggests an acceptance of racism which Meena has not been aware of.
   - First-person narrative gives empathy to Meena and the reader shares her growing awareness.
   - References to *To Kill a Mockingbird*, and the marked similarity of the ending to that novel's ending.

9. *The Woman in Black*
   - In the extract Arthur sees a woman in the graveyard.
   - He explains away what he sees to himself.

- Mr Jerome's reaction is unexpected as it shows that he is afraid.
- Mr Jerome does not discuss the woman with Arthur, leaving him puzzled. Readers would question Arthur's 'logical' explanation.
- The narrator has been introduced as being intelligent, sensible and sceptical.
- The sense of the supernatural is built through rumours.
- The use of unexplained noises, building to unexplained sights.
- Atmospheric descriptions of the landscape.
- Solving the mystery and understanding the woman's motives does not prevent her from harming Arthur Kipps.
- Sense that supernatural forces cannot be defeated or appeased.

10. *Oranges Are not the Only Fruit*
- The extract focuses on the visit of her natural mother.
- This is of huge significance but is not described in detail.
- Readers are left wondering what exactly has been said.
- It is told almost 'by the way' as a flashback in a chapter about other events.
- The reactions of both Jeanette and her mother are equally emotional.
- Why does Jeanette accept that it should be left in the past?
- Jeanette's identity initially comes from her adopted mother and her religion.
- As she grows up she finds a sense of identity through education and relationships.
- The fairy tale/fantasy elements of the novel are about searching for meaning and identity.

Page 57 English Literature Component 2

Section B: 19th-Century Prose

Look at the mark scheme below, decide which description is closest to your answer and then decide which mark to give yourself up to a maximum of **[40]**.

Marks	Skills
32–40	• You have sustained focus on the task, including an overview, and conveyed your ideas consistently and coherently. • You have approached the text sensitively and analysed it critically. • You have shown a perceptive understanding of the text, engaging with a personal response and some originality. • You have included pertinent quotations from the text. • You have analysed and appreciated the writer's use of language, form and structure. • You have used precise subject terminology appropriately. • You have shown an assured understanding of the relationship between the text and the context in which it was written.
24–31	• You have sustained focus on the task, including an overview, and conveyed your ideas coherently. • You have approached the text thoughtfully. • You have shown a secure understanding of key aspects of the text, with considerable engagement. • You have included well-chosen quotations from the text. • You have discussed and increasingly analysed the writer's use of language, form and structure. • You have used subject terminology appropriately. • You have shown a secure understanding of the relationship between the text and the context in which it was written.

[Maximum 40 marks]

Your answers could include some of the following points:

11. *The Strange Case of Dr Jekyll and Mr Hyde*
- The story is told by Poole, introducing another narrator.
- Another piece of the jigsaw for Utterson and the reader.
- Poole very close to Jekyll but is convinced it is not Jekyll.
- Poole's reaction is one of fear, his hair standing up – feels he has seen something evil.
- Compares the man he saw to a rat – Hyde is often compared to animals. He is also referred to as 'it', as if he is no longer human.
- Jekyll has physically shrunk – 'more of a dwarf' – matching other descriptions of Hyde.
- Stevenson is building up gradually to a full description of transformation.
- Utterson and others assume Hyde is a separate person. They see Jekyll as 'good'.
- Consider Dr Lanyon's narrative and his reaction.
- Consider Jekyll's own narrative and his motivation – to separate good and evil.
- The story shows that this is impossible – what else does it say about good and evil?

12. *A Christmas Carol*
- Here Dickens uses shock and horror, surprising the reader at the end of the chapter.
- The two children are personifications of Ignorance and Want (poverty).
- The language used to describe them is vivid and repulsive.
- However, the description is not very much exaggerated – it is what very poor children would look like.
- The ghost uses them as a warning of what might happen if poverty and lack of education are not dealt with – revolution.
- Dickens uses Scrooge's transformation to explore ideas about responsibility.
- Using the Christmas ghost story, a popular form, Dickens gets his messages across in an entertaining way.
- Being charitable and socially responsible is part of the spirit of Christmas – it does not stop you enjoying yourself.
- This chapter shows a wide range of people at Christmas, many poor.
- The Cratchits are used to show what life is like for poor families and how easy it could be to improve their lives.

13. *Jane Eyre*
- As narrator Jane shares the feelings she had at the time with the reader.
- Here she analyses her feelings, which she does throughout the novel.
- She opens with a rhetorical question and answers it.
- She analyses Rochester's character, calling him 'proud, sardonic, harsh' but also listing his good qualities.
- She is concerned with morality. It is important for her to think he is no longer immoral.
- It is now clear that she is in love with him, a feeling that has been developing throughout the novel.
- Jane rescues Rochester on several occasions – almost as if he has to be less powerful for her to love him.
- Symbolism of the fire and Rochester's attitude to Jane after it.
- His marriage to Bertha and his deception – Jane's reasons for leaving Thornfield.
- Jane's return to Thornfield and their mutual love.

14. *Pride and Prejudice*
- Contrast in reactions of Mr and Mrs Bennet.
- Elizabeth's reasons for rejecting Mr Collins.
- Ironic/comic tone of passage.
- Use of dialogue to convey attitudes of Mr and Mrs Bennet and their characters.
- Serious point given to unlikely character to make in a comic way. Who will maintain her if she is not married?
- Contrast Elizabeth's refusal with Charlotte Lucas's acceptance of Mr Collins.
- Marriage must be for love but must also make sense financially and socially.

- Other examples of marriage: Mr and Mrs Bennet, Lydia and Wickham, Jane and Bingley.
- Marriage of Elizabeth and Darcy as an ideal.

15. *Silas Marner*
- Silas's condition means he has not seen the child arrive and we see the discovery through his eyes.
- At first, he thinks it is his missing gold, the most important thing in his life.
- When he sees the child, he thinks it might be his dead sister, stirring feelings of love.
- The word 'mystery' is used at first in a religious sense, relating to the idea of a 'Power' sending her.
- At the end it is a mystery to be solved as he starts to think logically.
- He tries to help her but his 'dull bachelor mind' is not used to children.
- Eppie helps him to rediscover feelings (and the faith) he had lost.
- She brings him closer to the community as others offer to help.
- She replaces gold in his affections.
- He is rewarded when she chooses him over her natural father.

16. *War of the Worlds*
- The curate, like others, tries to make sense of the invasion.
- He sees it as a punishment from God, referring to the Bible and wondering what he and others have done to deserve it.
- His biblical language contrasts with the mundane details of suburban life in Weybridge (the Sunday school etc.)
- The narrator, while not rejecting God, rejects this idea using logic and humour: 'He is not an insurance agent'.
- Like many others, the curate feels helpless and is astonished that one of 'God's ministers' has been killed.
- The narrator's reaction changes as he experiences the invasion.
- He observes curiosity, panic, defiance and despair.
- Contrast the artilleryman's considered view with the curate's.

Page 63 English Literature Component 2

Section C: Unseen Poetry

17. Look at the mark scheme below, decide which description is closest to your answer and then decide which mark to give yourself. Part a) is marked out of **15** and part b) out of **25**. Total maximum mark **[40]**.

Marks	Skills
(a) 13–15 (b) 21–25	• You have sustained focus on the task, including an overview, and conveyed your ideas consistently and coherently. • You have approached the text sensitively and analysed it critically. • You have shown a perceptive understanding of the text, engaging with a personal response and some originality. • You have included pertinent quotations from the text. • You have analysed and appreciated the writer's use of language, form and structure. • You have used precise subject terminology appropriately. • You have shown an assured understanding of the relationships between texts and the contexts in which they were written. • (part b) only) You have made critical and illuminating comparisons throughout. • (part b) only) There is a wide ranging discussion of the similarities and differences.
(a) 10–12 (b) 16–20	• You have sustained focus on the task, including an overview, and conveyed your ideas coherently. • You have approached the text thoughtfully. • You have shown a secure understanding of key aspects of the text, with considerable engagement. • You have included well-chosen quotations from the text. • You have discussed and increasingly analysed the writer's use of language, form and structure. • You have used subject terminology appropriately. • You have shown a secure understanding of the relationships between texts and the contexts in which they were written. • (part b) only) You have made focussed and coherent comparisons throughout. • (part b) only) There is a clear discussion of the similarities and differences.

Your answer might include comments on the following:

a)
- Poem in three regular stanzas.
- Impact of short rhyming couplet in lines 5 and 6 of each stanza.
- It starts with a grand, general statement and then gives examples.
- The third stanza addresses the reader directly.
- Death is a 'leveller' because it is the same for everyone and all are equal.
- Personification of Death ('his icy hand').
- Identification of classes of people by things associated with them ('Sceptre and Crown', 'scythe and spade') – called 'metonymy' in literary criticism.
- The poem reads like a warning.
- The language reflects decay: 'dust', 'wither'.
- There are many words associated with surrender and powerlessness: 'tumble', 'yield', 'stoop', 'captives'.
- For most of the poem the tone is negative – it seems as if no human activity is worthwhile as it all ends in death.
- The last two lines give hope of a kind, an idea that 'the just' can leave something behind.

b)
- The first is about death in general, the second about the death of an individual.
- Stevenson speaks of how he would like to be remembered; Shirley implies no-one will be remembered.
- Stevenson expresses contentment with both life and death. Shirley's view of death is not comforting.
- Both focus on what remains; the grave; the dust.
- Rhythm, rhyme and alliteration give Stevenson's poem a cheerful tone. Shirley's is more ponderous, with a heavy beat.
- Both have stanzas of equal length, but Shirley's are more complex, as is what he is saying.
- The rhyme schemes are also regular in both poems – again, Stevenson's is simpler.
- Both poets use the second person, 'you', but for Stevenson 'you' seems to be a loved one, while for Shirley it is anyone who reads the poem.
- Stevenson's idea of death being like coming home contrasts with Shirley's focus on the 'cold tomb'.
- Shirley's poem reads like a warning, inspiring fear and guilt, whereas Stevenson seeks to comfort the reader.

Notes

Notes

Acknowledgements

The author and publisher are grateful to the copyright holders for permission to use quoted materials and images.

All images © Shutterstock.com

P.26 *Death of A Naturalist* by Seamus Heaney from New and Selected Poems 1966-1967 (2002) Reprinted by permission of the publishers, Faber and Faber Ltd.

P.26 Cozy Apologia. Copyright © 2004 by Rita Dove, from COLLECTED POEMS: 1974-2004 by Rita Dove. Used by permission of W. W. Norton & Company, Inc.

P.52 © Willy Russell, 2001, *Blood Brothers*. Reprinted by permission of Methuen Drama, an imprint of Bloomsbury Publishing Plc.

P.52 From AN INSPECTOR CALLS by J.B. Priestley (Penguin Books, 2001) Copyright © J.B. Priestley, 1947.

P.53 © Simon Stephens, 2004, *The Curious Incident of the Dog in the Night-Time*. Reprinted by permission of Methuen Drama, an imprint of Bloomsbury Publishing Plc.

P.53 *The History Boys* by Alan Bennett (2004) Faber and Faber Ltd.

P.54 *Lord of the Flies* by William Golding (1954) Reprinted by permission of the publishers, Faber and Faber Ltd.

P.54 © Shelagh Delaney, 1982, *A Taste of Honey*. Reprinted by permission of Methuen Drama, an imprint of Bloomsbury Publishing Plc.

P.55 *Anita and Me* Reprinted by permission of HarperCollins Publishers Ltd © 1997 Meera Syal

P.55 *Never Let Me Go* by Kazuo Ishiguro (2010) Reprinted by permission of the publishers, Faber and Faber Ltd.

P.56 From *The Woman in Black* by Susan Hill published by Vintage. Reproduced by permission of The Random House Group Ltd. ©1992

P.56 From *Oranges Are Not the Only Fruit* by Jeanette Winterson published by Vintage. Reproduced by permission of The Random House Group Ltd. ©1991

Every effort has been made to trace copyright holders and obtain their permission for the use of copyright material. The author and publisher will gladly receive information enabling them to rectify any error or omission in subsequent editions. All facts are correct at time of going to press.

Published by Collins
An imprint of HarperCollins*Publishers* Ltd
1 London Bridge Street
London SE1 9GF

HarperCollins*Publishers*
Macken House, 39/40 Mayor Street Upper,
Dublin 1, D01 C9W8, Ireland

© HarperCollins*Publishers* Limited 2020

ISBN 9780008326920

Content first published 2018
This edition published 2020

10 9 8 7 6 5 4 3

British Library Cataloguing in Publication Data.

A CIP record of this book is available from the British Library.

Author: Paul Burns
Commissioning Editors: Clare Souza and Kerry Ferguson
Editor and Project Manager: Katie Galloway
Cover Design: Sarah Duxbury and Kevin Robbins
Inside Concept Design: Sarah Duxbury and Paul Oates
Text Design and Layout: Jouve India Private Limited
Production: Lyndsey Rogers
Printed in the UK, by Ashford Colour Press Ltd.

MIX
Paper | Supporting responsible forestry
FSC www.fsc.org FSC™ C007454

This book contains FSC™ certified paper and other controlled sources to ensure responsible forest management.

For more information visit: www.harpercollins.co.uk/green